Pelican Books

Almost Everyone's Guide

D0685108

John Kenneth Galbraith was American Ambassador to India from 1961–3, and for many years Paul M. Warburg Professor of Economics at Harvard University. He was born in 1908 in Canada, on a farm at Iona Station, Ontario. After graduating in agriculture at Toronto and taking a PhD at the University of California, he became Social Science Research Council Fellow at Cambridge, England, and has taught at the Universities of California and Princeton as well as at Harvard from 1945 to 1975. In 1970–71 he spent two terms at Cambridge University as Fellow at Trinity College and Visiting Lecturer at the Faculty of Economics and Politics.

During the war, at the American Office of Price Administration, he headed the wartime price control activities, and later was a director of the US Strategic Bombing Survey and of the Office of Security Policy, receiving the Medal of Freedom and the President's Certificate of Merit for his work. He has been closely identified with the Democratic Party.

Professor Galbraith is well known as a contributor to leading American journals and reviews. His books include: *A Theory of Price Control*, *American Capitalism*, *The Affluent Society* (which held its place on the best-seller lists for some thirty weeks), *The Great Crash 1929*, *The Liberal Hour*, *The Non-potable Scotch*, *The New Industrial State*, and *Economics, Peace and Laughter*. He is also the author of a book of satirical sketches, *The McLandress Dimension*, the best-selling novel, *The Triumph*, (with M. S. Randhawa) a study of Indian painting, *Indian Painting; Scene, Themes and Legends*, *Ambassador's Journal*, *A China Passage*, a record of his visit to China, *Economics and the Public Purpose*, *Money: Whence It Came, Where It Went*, *The Age of Uncertainty* and *The Nature of Mass Poverty*. He delivered the Reith Lectures in 1966.

Professor Galbraith, who is an enthusiastic skier, is married and has three sons. Much of his writing has been done in Switzerland and on an old farm in Vermont.

For Pierre Mendès-France
with admiration

Contents

Acknowledgements

Edith Tucker typed this manuscript and could have been the most comprehensively over-qualified person recently so engaged. While doing it, she also scrutinized the ideas and ran a hard and successful campaign for her local school committee. To Edith thanks; to the children of Wellesley, Massachusetts, congratulations. Emmy Davis, a colleague and friend of several seasons, did all the things that allow me to write (or otherwise accomplish) books, including much that I simply find more pleasant to leave to her. Phyllis Turner, in earlier times my assistant but now lost to a husband and NATO, came from Brussels to the Loire to transcribe the tapes of these conversations, a most friendly act. Andrea Williams, as so often before, corrected, improved, edited and otherwise protected a reputation for grammar, syntax, punctuation and expression that I do not deserve. Catherine Galbraith listened to all of these conversations and, if Nicole Salinger seemed too easily satisfied, which was not often, demanded further clarification. To all more thanks and much love in which Nicole warmly joins.

JKG

Foreword

We've been friends for a long time, and we are both friends of Jean Lacouture, the truly wise author and editor who came to much deserved prominence in both France and the United States with his searching journalism on Vietnam. For some years now, for Éditions du Seuil, Jean has been arranging interviews of assorted writers and scholars similar to the one in this book.

Or partly so. Most often the interviewers have sought to explore in depth the life and background or the soul of the artist in question. The Galbraith soul, it was all too apparent, did not lend itself to such investigation. It is a shallow, pallid thing – one thinks of a disposable tissue – interesting only for the evidence of abuse and neglect. His life, so far as it hasn't been revealed in a journal, a novel and a book on his Canadian antecedents, is one day soon to be recaptured in a separate work, quite possibly of undue length and self-enhancement. There remained only economics.

As we considered it, this seemed the best subject of all. Economics pre-empts the headlines. It bears on everyone's life, anxieties and, if more rarely, satisfactions. Its subject matter – more precisely, the circumstances with which it deals – is in a state of rapid change, one that, all too obviously, has left the statesmen and their advisers who apply its solutions well behind. This must be so; were it otherwise, they couldn't promise an end to inflation, an end to unemployment and then often achieve an increase in both. So we proposed to Jean that we try to see if the state of economics in general, and the reasons for its present failure in particular, might not be put in simple, accurate language that almost everyone could understand and that a perverse few might conceivably enjoy. It would be a conversation or, more specifically, a well-considered line of questioning in which any literate person might have participated.

We began the interrogation in the Loire Valley in September of 1977 and continued it during the autumn in Switzerland and Cambridge. The first result of our talks was usually far from complete or clear. When this was so, we amended and revised or did it over.

The economist provided the economics, and it will occur to some perceptive students of the obvious that this is Galbraith's view of economic life and not that, or not yet that, of the wholly conventional men and tracts. So it is. But were the current orthodoxies reliable and the policies they advocate applicable, we wouldn't be in the trouble we are in. We have seen the present, and it doesn't work. No economist can claim a monopoly of truth. But in what is now believed, given the results, there is a presumption of error.

If a question is asked that has been asked before, there is a certain likelihood that the answer will be similar or the same. A commitment to the same answer after the underlying conditions have greatly, even drastically, changed is a major source of error in economics, as this discussion amply avers. But consistency is not, universally, a sin. Some of the questions here asked have been asked before. What is true must be repeated. The inevitable may be more tolerable if confessed.

As Galbraith is responsible for the economics, so Nicole is responsible for its accessibility. Her function was not only to question but to persist: 'Your point doesn't come clear.' 'It still doesn't.' Many years ago, George Bernard Shaw wrote a small classic, *The Intelligent Woman's Guide to Capitalism and Socialism*. Our book, Nicole Salinger being of that race, might have been called *The Intelligent Frenchwoman's Guide to Economics and Economists*. But brevity is a virtue as élitism is not. So we threw open the door to the whole available audience:

Almost Everyone's Guide to Economics. If the guidance is any-where obscure, it is Nicole's fault. Though she persisted, she didn't persist enough.

JKG
NS

Chapter 1

What Is Economics Anyway?

NICOLE SALINGER: *Winston Churchill said he could understand almost anything else but could not get his mind around economics. And yet obviously it is very important. What is economics exactly? And can I get my mind around it?*

JOHN KENNETH GALBRAITH: As to the last, certainly. And on essentials Churchill could, too. Let me remind you of the rest of his statement. He said he couldn't get his mind around economics, but he did know that shooting Montagu Norman would be a good thing. Montagu Norman was then the head of the Bank of England.

Alfred Marshall, the great Cambridge economist who dominated the accepted British – and American – economic teaching from the 1880s to the 1920s, said that economics is merely the study of mankind in the ordinary business of life. I would now add a reference to organization – to the study of the way people are organized for economic tasks by corporations, by trade unions and by government. Also of how and when and to what extent organizations serve their own purposes as opposed to those of the people at large. And of how the public purposes can be made to prevail.

NICOLE: *When I understand economics, what can it do for me? Anything?*

JKG: To have a working understanding of economics is to understand the largest part of life. We pass our years, most of us, contemplating the relationship between the money we earn and the money we need, our thoughts suspended, as it were, between the two. Economics is about what we earn and what we can get for it. So an understanding of economics is an understanding of life's principal preoccupation.

There is another thing it can do for you. The newspaper headlines, when they escape from sex and the Middle East, are largely concerned with the economic decisions of governments. If people make no effort to understand these decisions, do not have an intelligent position and do not make that position known, they obviously surrender all power to those who do understand, pretend to understand or believe they understand. And you can be sure that the decisions so made will rarely be damaging to those who make them or to the people they represent.

NICOLE: *Valéry Giscard d'Estaing said in his recent book that economics is like the human body, an automatic regulatory mechanism and a further decision taken by the brain. Is that so?*

JKG: All similes for economic life should be resisted, but this is better than most. There are aspects of economic life which are still self-regulating, although they are diminishing in relation to the whole. And there are aspects which require guidance. It's the issues in this guidance – who is favored and who isn't – that the citizen and voter must understand.

Do you think we've now persuaded all susceptible people that they should have a working knowledge of economics?

NICOLE: *I'm persuaded, all right. But why don't more people try?*

JKG: Partly they are put off by the terminology. We economists protect ourselves from outsiders by resort to a language of our own. People in all professions do it to some extent. Physicians have their own language, as do lawyers and psychiatrists and burglars, I'm told. All like to see themselves as a priestly class with a knowledge, a mystique, that isn't available to the everyday citizen.

And some people, maybe many, are deterred by the feeling that current economic explanations are at odds with everyday reality. They hear an economist say, in describing how prices are set, that he assumes pure competition – the competition of many small firms in the market. And in the real world they see only a few vast enterprises supplying the gasoline, automobiles, chemicals, pharmaceuticals, electricity, telephone services or what have you. So they say to hell with it – economics isn't my world.

NICOLE: *Economists don't all agree; many totally disagree. Why do they disagree? How do I tell whom I should believe?*

JKG: You should believe me, of course. As to the disagreement, there are several reasons. There is self-interest, something we all recognize and are usually too polite to mention. An economist who works for a large New York bank rarely comes up with a conclusion that is adverse to the interest of his bank as that is understood by his employers. His public truth is what gains their approval. There has always been in the United States a healthy suspicion of the views of the economics professor who has a remunerative consulting relationship with corporations. Certainly his view will be different from that of an economist who is employed by a trade union.

Political identification also makes for disagreement. In the United States we have Republican economists and Democratic economists. Their personal politics controls or shapes their conclusions. That has been true in my case; over the years I've found virtue, at election time, in the views of some Democrats of exceptional illiteracy, economically speaking.

Quite a few economists measure their truth by the applause it evokes; they adjust their position, perhaps unconsciously, to what their audience will think agreeable.

Then, more important and perhaps more to be forgiven, there is the problem of change. The ultimate subject matter of the physical sciences is fixed. That of economics, in contrast, is always in the process of change – the corporation, the labor force, the behavior of the consumer, the role of government, are all always in transition. This means that economics, if it is to avoid obsolescence, must adapt in two ways. It must change as new information is added or interpretation is improved. And it must change as basic institutions change. Disagreement then comes because different economists have different reactions to change. Some yearn to believe that the basic subject matter, like that of the hard sciences, is given for all time. Some accept that economic institutions are in a process of continual alteration – that what was true of corporate, trade union, consumer or government behavior yesterday will not be true today and certainly not tomorrow.

There are still other reasons for disagreement. Some economists are very economical of thought and bring the lessons of their profession into their personal lives. They seek, accordingly, to make any ideas, once acquired, last a lifetime. A measure of disagreement comes, I suppose, from some being more intelligent than others, although that, too, is a thought that all decent and modest scholars suppress.

There isn't much difficulty in telling who has an ax to grind; our oldest instinct is to ask who is paying. Also, if an economist gets too much applause from the affluent, you should always be suspicious. The rich in all countries combine a fairly acute self-interest with an ever-present feeling of anxiety and guilt. Anyone who relieves that anxiety and guilt is assured of applause, and seeking that applause, not the truth, easily becomes a habit. Beyond that, the only test is to ask for the fullest possible explanation, then ask yourself whether the explanation is truly complete and makes sense. If an economist ever suggests that you take something on faith because of his or her professional knowledge, dismiss him or her forthwith from your thoughts.

NICOLE: *There is reference to 'economics', and also to 'political economy'. Does it become political economy when the government assumes a critical function and role?*

JKG: That would be logical, as you French require. In fact, political economy is the older term. In the early professional discussion of the subject in Britain – that started by Adam Smith with *Wealth of Nations* in 1776 and continued by David Ricardo, Thomas Robert Malthus and John Stuart Mill in the first half of the last century – the reference was to political economy. No sharp line was drawn between the role of the consumer and business firm on the one hand and that of the state on the other. All were seen as part of one great system.

Then, toward the end of the last century, the term 'economics' came into use. It reflected a more virginal view of the subject, from which the government was largely excluded. Producers and consumers came together in the market; the market was the all-powerful regulatory force in society. All important needs were so supplied. The state had only a minor and often rather derogatory role. Economics was political economy cleansed of politics.

In very recent times there has been an effort to revive the older term and bring the reference to political economy back into use. This, as you might suppose, is on the grounds that the distinction between economics and politics is now an artificial one, that government has a necessary and powerful influence on economic behavior and performance. Even the term 'political economy' is now misleadingly narrow in its connotations.

NICOLE: *If you can't separate economics from politics, can you separate it from philosophy, history, sociology, demography, geography – I suppose not from pornography. Don't they all bear on economic understanding?*

JKG: All distinctions – all lines of separation – are artificial. If something influences economic behavior, then it is important for economics. You mentioned demography – the dynamics of population growth. It's a vital matter, especially for understanding economic life in the poor countries. And demography leads on to biology, family structure, social preferences and compulsions. All bear upon the rate of population increase and the economic result. An economist can't know everything. But neither can he exclude anything.

NICOLE: *Coming back to economics: is it the same for all countries – the United States, France, Britain, India, Algeria? Do the same rules hold in the Soviet Union, Poland, Yugoslavia? Or is there a different economics – or political economy – for each country?*

JKG: Certainly there are differences. But there is a broad resemblance between countries at the same stage in development. Certainly as between the United States, Britain and France the similarities are very much greater than the differences. All make steel, automobiles, chemicals, numerous other products, on a large scale. For such manufacture, inevitably, you have very large corporations. And in all large corporations the structure of organization is much the same. Also all bring trade unions into existence; given the power of the corporation as a buyer and user of labor, it occurs to workers that they must, of necessity, have unions as a form of countervailing power.

In addition, large corporations make similar demands on government for essential services, qualified manpower, research and development, financial rescue when they get in trouble. And as some industries lend themselves only to large-scale organization, others – agriculture, consumer services, artistic effort – operate best with smaller units. What is necessary in France is required also in the United States. So there is a basic structural similarity as between the developed industrial economies. And this similarity extends in a general way to the socialist countries – to the Soviet Union and Eastern Europe. There, too, the large-scale production of steel, automobiles or chemicals requires large organizations. Agriculture works best in smaller units. Artists work by themselves. These differences in organization shape the character of the society.

NICOLE: *What about planning?*

JKG: The socialist economies are planned. The need for materials and components is foreseen and related to the intended production of finished goods. The aggregate of income is related, if imperfectly, to what there will be to buy, none of this being as simple as it sounds. But there is also much planning in the non-socialist countries – by corporations to ensure the supply of steel and components for the automobiles they will produce; by their marketing men to ensure that consumers will want the new automobile design when it appears; and by the government to provide highways on which the cars can be driven, to ensure gasoline to propel them and also the purchasing power to buy them. Though devout free-enterprisers suppress the thought, all modern industrial economies are extensively planned. They must be.

NICOLE: *What about the Third World countries?*

JKG: The great difference in economic organization is between the rich countries and the poor countries. The poor countries, because they are poor, are primarily concerned with the necessaries of life: food, clothing, shelter. These are mostly produced by small firms with a simple structure – one man, a family. Being small, the individual producer is without power. The firms being numerous, he is much more subject to the impersonal forces of the market. Producers in the poor countries also have fewer needs from the state, and government services play a smaller part in living standards. In all everyday discussion we exaggerate the differences in economic structure of the United States and the Soviet Union. And we greatly underestimate the differences between the economic systems of, say, the United States and India or of France and her former African colonies.

NICOLE: *Aren't there countries in between, countries which still are considered undeveloped in the general character of their production and consumption but which have some highly technical or mass production industry, sometimes based on a primary resource? I think of Iran, for instance.*

JKG: Yes. This is a needed correction of my generalization. Even in the poorest countries, such as Iran or India, there are highly developed islands of industry – petrochemicals in Iran, steel in India. And the structure there, in turn, is very similar to that of the same industries in the developed countries. There is no difference that need detain us between Aramco in Saudi Arabia and Texaco in the United States.

NICOLE: *Let me go on to another subject. Can economists tell what will happen in the future? Did they predict the oil crisis?*

JKG: Maybe someone did. But no one paid attention. And rightly, for there was no way of knowing he was prescient. In fact, there are very great limits to what economists can predict. We must be judged by what we explain and what results from the policies we urge, not by what we foretell as to the stock market or the price of oil. You must always remember that prediction itself derives from the fact that no one knows. If something can be known, as for example that the sun will rise tomorrow morning and at exactly 6:24.24, then no one predicts it, not even on television.

Remember, too, that official economic prediction is not meant to be right; it only tells what governments need to have happen. A high government economist never predicts that unemployment will continue and get worse, that inflation will continue and accelerate and that the budget deficit will eventually be the highest on record. Any chairman of the Council of Economic Advisers in Washington who unleashed that kind of news would get an urgent message from the Oval Office. Yet, sadly enough, unemployment, inflation and the deficit do very often increase.

I should add that many economists make predictions, especially around Christmastime for the new year, not because they know what will happen but because they get asked. It's a ritual.

The safe rule for the citizen on economic predictions is to ignore them.

NICOLE: *I want to ask you later on about inflation and unemployment. But should we have a definition of them now?*

JKG: There is no mystery. Inflation is steadily rising prices – not some going up, others going down, but all or most going up together. This, needless to say, includes wages and salaries, at least of the fortunate. Our great definition of unemployment comes down to us from Calvin Coolidge. He said, 'When a great many people are out of work, unemployment results.' You got similar wisdom, I believe, from Monsieur de la Palisse.

NICOLE: *What is the definition of economic growth? Why do people talk about it so much? Why does every politician praise himself for the growth he has achieved – or will achieve?*

JKG: Economic growth is merely an increase – a more than momentary increase – in the output of all the things we consume, use, invest in or otherwise produce. Economic growth and increasing production are the same thing.

NICOLE: *Is that the same as increasing Gross National Product – GNP?*

JKG: Yes, the Gross National Product is the value, in current prices or those of some past time, of everything that is produced and sold in the course of the year. It includes, of course, the value at cost of all public services.

NICOLE: *And what is the National Income?*

JKG: Nearly the same thing, in practice. Everything that is produced and sold returns income to somebody. From the sale somebody gets a profit, a wage, a salary or, if no profit, a loss that is a gain to someone else. The value of the product is one side of the account, the income the other side of the same account. Gross National Product and National Income are not, in fact, quite equal; some things go into the value of a product that don't come out as income. That needn't bother us, at least today.

NICOLE: *Why are the GNP and National Income so important, both of them?*

JKG: In the years following the Second World War, economic growth, meaning the increase in Gross National Product, became the test of national economic performance and to some extent of national virtue. A country was known to be doing well or badly in accordance with its percentage rate of annual increase in GNP.

I never tire of my own aphorisms: eventually it came to pass that when economists and politicians presented themselves at the Holy Gate, Saint Peter asked only what they had done to increase the GNP. Japan was the greatest success in this period because it had the greatest increase in Gross National Product. The British were the wretched of the earth because of their low annual increase in GNP.

You ask why it is important. In fact, Gross National Product has been oversold.

NICOLE: *That is because not everything is included?*

JKG: Partly. Only things that are readily measurable are included in the Gross National Product. I work in a very leisurely way as befits a Harvard professor, but my production, measured by my salary, is included in the Gross National Product of the United States. My wife works very hard managing our family and household, but, since she doesn't get a wage, she doesn't get included. Economists could get a very sudden increase in the GNP by discovering and including the unpaid labor of women.

There is another oddity having to do with sex. A woman of the street, since she charges for her affection, contributes to Gross National Product, at least in principle. A lovely and loving mistress does not.

More seriously, a city that plans its growth properly, manages its parks well and has clean, safe streets can have a lower contribution to the GNP than a city that does none of these things but produces and sells a lot of goods. You brought up pornography. A busy shop selling dirty pictures does more for the GNP than the absence of air pollution.

NICOLE: *Is it because the enjoyment from good city planning, pleasant parks, safe streets, cannot be measured? They are like true love?*

JKG: That is why they are excluded. And it's quite arbitrary. Many unmeasurable things have a greater human reward than measurable things.

NICOLE: *Including the arts?*

JKG: Arts, love, enjoyment of one's surroundings, nice highways that wind through the countryside without a great clutter of advertising. All these things give a great deal of pleasure but aren't included in the Gross National Product.

NICOLE: *I've heard it said that rather than talk about a Gross National Product we should talk about a Gross National Happiness. Should we not have a measure of the quality of life rather than the quantity of goods?*

JKG: There have been efforts in that direction – to include values associated with social contentment and enjoyment. They haven't been very successful – again, the problem of measurement. One reason the British have had a low increase in Gross National Product is that they take a larger part of their return in the unmeasurable rewards. They have the best-maintained countryside in Europe, much better certainly than the United States has, better even than that in France. They have good public services. It is much easier and more pleasant to commute into London than into New York. Recreational facilities, parks, playing fields, are far better arranged and looked after in London than in New York. So one can easily argue that the average Londoner has a lower per capita GNP but a higher standard of well-being than the average New Yorker.

Still, there is a beloved economic cliché: do not throw out the baby with the bathwater unless it's a very dirty baby indeed. The Gross National Product does not measure the quality of life. But it does tell us something useful about the trend in the production of goods and services. We should use it for what it tells us so long as we know what it doesn't tell us.

NICOLE: *May I become more technical? Economists talk about microeconomics and macroeconomics. Could you explain?*

JKG: You are not becoming all that technical – nothing that would impress Professor Samuelson or your Professor Malinvaud.

Microeconomics is the branch of economics that deals with the firm and the household, the ultimate cellular structure; thus the overtones of microscope and microbiology. It then goes on to deal with the market – to tell, or anyhow imagine, how consumers, given their income and preferences, interact through the market with business firms to determine what is produced, in what amount, at what profit and at what price.

Macroeconomics became a separate topic of discussion and was so named in the aftermath of John Maynard Keynes and the Great Depression. It then came generally to be realized that consumers and business firms might not have enough spendable income or might not spend or invest enough from their income to buy all the goods and services that could be produced. There would, as a consequence, be idle plant capacity and unemployment. Or, though it was not a problem during the Depression, people and governments might spend in excess of the productive capacity of the economy. Then there would be inflation – one kind of inflation.

So it became a function of government to regulate the overall or aggregate relationships between all buyers and all sellers. This meant providing more purchasing power and more demand when that was indicated, restricting purchasing power and demand when that was called for. The expansion was accomplished by lowering taxes or increasing public expenditures or encouraging borrowing from the banks and consequent spending for business investment, housing or automobiles. Restriction was achieved by putting all these actions in reverse. Such is macroeconomic policy.

I might add that the distinction between microeconomics and macroeconomics, though still greatly cherished by economists in setting up courses and examining doctoral candidates, is no longer useful in real life. More likely it is now a barrier to understanding. That is because the line between microeconomics and macroeconomics becomes very blurred in a time when corporations can raise their prices and trade unions can increase their wages. These actions, as much as an excess of purchasing power, have become a cause of inflation. And unemployment is now the normal consequence of the effort to keep corporations, trade unions and others from increasing their prices and wages by cutting back on demand. So both inflation and unemployment are now as much or more a consequence of microeconomic phenomena as of macroeconomic policy. In economics artificial divisions of the subject matter – specialization – can be a prime source of error. Economic truth only emerges when things are examined whole.

NICOLE: *Inflation and unemployment are surely the paramount issues of our time. Every country is struggling with them. Why?*

JKG: We talked of change. Before I can answer your question, we must see how underlying conditions have changed and how the ideas that interpret those conditions have lagged behind.

NICOLE: *One final question for today. Is this combination of inflation and unemployment what some economists call stagflation?*

JKG: Yes. But it's a term I do not use. One has to draw the line. There are some additions to the English language that are too wretched.

Chapter 2

The Economic Systems

NICOLE: *How would you describe the economic system which you say is common to the industrial countries, the non-socialist countries, such as the United States, Britain, Germany, France?*

JKG: Well, it goes under various names. In France it's called the liberal economic system. But liberal means conservative in France while in the United States a liberal is to the left and an ultra-liberal is dangerously to the left. The standard American and British reference is to the neo-classical system. In any case, it's a set of ideas that owe their origin in the latter half of the eighteenth century to Adam Smith and, in some measure, to the French Physiocrats – Quesnay, Turgot and Du Pont, the first of the chemical dynasty. The Physiocrats shared many of Adam Smith's beliefs but were persuaded that there was special merit in agricultural development. The original ideas were four in number, and they are all still influential.

First, the motivating force or incentive in the economic system is self-interest. This guides people to serve the common interest as though, Adam Smith said, by an invisible hand.

Second, the system is regulated by competition – the competition of many firms in each line of production or trade. Prices are established by competition; all firms are subordinate to the market prices so established; none can influence the prices in the market. That would be to regulate the regulator. I should say, more than parenthetically, that Adam Smith detected a dismaying tendency for sellers to combine in order to raise prices and thus destroy this regulatory power of the market. He was also very suspicious of joint stock companies, now called corporations, which, besides being strongly inclined to monopoly, he also thought not very efficient. He would have allowed them only for a limited range of large tasks. Many people who now yearn to resurrect Smith will find him a scathing enemy if they succeed.

Third, given the regulatory power of competition, there need be little regulation by the state. The latter should be as small and unobtrusive and inexpensive as the requirements of law and order and the common defense allow.

Fourth and finally, since competition and the market bring the best possible results, you want as much of both as possible. The greater the trading area, the more competition and the stronger the market. Also, the greater the opportunity for specialization – division of labor – the greater the efficiency. So this is a system which argues strongly for free trade. This was the founding or classical design.

NICOLE: *Why then neo-classical instead of classical?*

JKG: There was much further refinement – and change. Economists have a passion for refinement. It is also a useful source of employment. And the ability to know and understand the refinements is our test of whether an economics student is a genius or only a near-genius. Anyhow, the reference to neo-classical economics became general early in this century. It emphasized, among other things, the idea of marginality. This held that the consumer in the market spreads his or her purchases around among different products and different services so that the added satisfaction from an additional dollar or franc, wherever spent, is equal. Everyone remembers from the economics textbooks about utility and its being equal at the margin. This was the optimal state of satisfaction or contentment to which all consumers had a tendency to proceed.

NICOLE: *Did this work on the production side, too?*

JKG: Yes. Neo-classical marginality held, similarly, that the business firm would extend its production up to the point where the cost of an additional unit of the product would be just equal to the revenue received for that product. Under competition, of course, that would be the price. Marginal cost would equal price. This was the optimal condition of efficiency to which all producers aspired.

So both consumption and production tended to be at the ideal level. Not quite, however, for the theory always glossed over the fact that the rich balanced their satisfactions at the margin with a lot more purchases than the poor. Total satisfaction, it might be thought, would be enhanced by taking some income from the rich and giving a little more to the poor. And also there was monopoly. With monopoly, additional production might lower prices. So here production would stop where marginal cost was equal to the return as reduced by the added production. This volume of production was less than the best. These refinements were variously formulated by Austrian, American and British economists. You will understand why those who taught these ideas weren't regarded as revolutionaries.

NICOLE: *Is this the same as the equilibrium system? And what is that exactly?*

JKG: A reference to equilibrium economics has the same connotation, more or less. The economic system was seen to resemble the pendulum of an unwound clock. It could be disturbed by many things, but it would always return to the same position – to the point where the consumer had maximized satisfaction with the best distribution of his or her expenditures and the producer was producing at the most efficient level of output, this being where marginal cost equaled price.

I should also add that everyone or almost everyone would be employed. For if someone were out of work, he would naturally cut his asking price for a job, give some producer a lower marginal cost and thus make worthwhile his employment.

This equilibrium would also come to exist between industries, for if wages and profits were higher in one industry than another, people and investment would move until competition had equalized return, made it the same everywhere. The idea of a general economic equilibrium was the specific refinement of Léon Walras, who lived from the 1830s until 1910 and who was the son of another famous economist, Auguste Walras. The younger Walras was a Frenchman and a failed mathematician. He went on to study as a mining engineer, then went on up, academically speaking, to economics and became a professor at the University of Lausanne. His general equilibrium was expressed mathematically, and he is regarded as one of the founders of mathematical economics, which shows you should always keep on trying.

The Walrasian view of the system depended, as did all neo-classical economics, on the competition of many small firms and so on the uninhibited rule of the market. Consumers and producers were, both and all, regulated by prices that none was large enough in the market to control. Monopoly was an exception but only an imperfection that did no general or decisive harm.

NICOLE: *The reality seems to me clearly different today. When was the neo-classical system dismissed from practical use?*

JKG: Well, with one important modification, it is still how many economists perceive reality. Or, more precisely, without their quite believing it, it is still what they teach to the young. The major modification came in the Great Depression. Then it was seen and accepted that the equilibrium could exist with a very great deal of unemployment. The equilibrium system was no longer thought to be quite the best in the best of all possible worlds.

NICOLE: *That was the contribution of Keynes?*

JKG: Yes, it was. John Maynard Keynes was the great hero of my generation. But it's always important to see first what Keynes didn't do. He did not attack the notion of the motivating power of self-interest. And he didn't attack the benign regulatory role of competition and the market. In Keynes's writing these ideas, this perception of reality, remained very largely intact. What he attacked, and very successfully, was the notion that the modern economy finds that equilibrium of which we have just spoken with all, or nearly all, willing workers employed. He held that it could find its equilibrium just as well with a very large amount of unemployment.

NICOLE: *Could you explain? You obviously need to.*

JKG: To explain, I must go back and pay tribute to another French economist, J. B. Say, who lived – I am looking it up – from 1767 to 1832. Say was the man who brought the ideas of Adam Smith to France. But he added a very important idea of his own, Say's Law of Markets. This held that whenever something was produced and sold, someone, of necessity, received in wages, profit or rent the wherewithal to buy that product. Every sale created the income and therewith the demand, in some form or other, for the product that was sold. Even if the recipients of profits or rents didn't spend what they received, their savings would be borrowed by someone else at some rate of interest. And if savings weren't borrowed, prices would fall so that purchasing power would still be sufficient. There would always thus be enough demand for the product. So there could never, never in the economic system be a shortage of purchasing power.

Say's Law, I must tell you, captured the economic mind as Lenin captured the revolutionaries of Russia. Until the middle of the 1930s – I do not exaggerate – no one could get a Ph.D. at Harvard if he didn't believe in Say's Law, assuming he were asked about so obvious a point. Later he might not get a Ph.D. at Harvard if he did believe in Say's Law, for it was Say's Law that Keynes destroyed. Keynes held that there could be a shortage of purchasing power. Individuals and business firms could save and not spend. And the equilibrium could be re-established not by falling prices but by falling production and increasing unemployment. These would reduce spending and investment, but they would reduce savings even more. The losses that firms incurred from doing business, plus the absolute necessity for spending by individuals (including spending from past savings) to keep alive, would so reduce net current savings that they would be brought in line with current investment, however low that might be. This was the grim and brutal way the neo-classical equilibrium was established.

Keynes, I should add, went on to the obvious prescription – the government should borrow and spend enough to offset any excess of savings at full employment. This became the Keynesian remedy, the final building block of the neo-classical system. It was published in 1936 in Keynes's great work, *The General Theory of Employment Interest and Money*. We soon came to speak of it lovingly as *The General Theory*. Actually, Keynes had advocated the remedy well before the justification was published in this book.

NICOLE: *So Keynes came out of the crisis. Is he obsolete today?*

JKG: Yes, although not all economists yet agree. His ideas are still those of the mainstream of western economics. Careful, intelligent or inspired management by the government and the central banks will supply the purchasing power that will keep employment at a high level without other adverse consequences; this is still the implicit faith of most economists in public office. But unfortunately you can be in high office and still be obsolete.

To be more specific, Keynes was concerned with unemployment and depression; he was almost completely unconcerned with inflation, which, in the years of his greatest contribution, was not troublesome. His system does not deal with it. And since inflation has been a central problem of the industrial countries for the last decade or more, any view of the economy that doesn't deal effectively with it can reasonably be called obsolete. As a first approximation to explaining our present difficulties, especially in the United States, it can be said that we are guided by people who have adopted Keynes's ideas but have not moved much beyond. Accordingly, they are without a remedy for inflation.

NICOLE: *If the Keynesian system is obsolete, does that mean that the present economy must be totally changed? Or can it be adapted to solve the new problem, the control of inflation?*

JKG: I've always believed that capitalism lends itself to more reform, more patching up of one messy sort or another, than most scholars of any intellectual rigor and purity imagine. Or businessmen, for that matter. Many businessmen believe that any modification of the system is destructive, the first step down to Bolshevism. One reason for my own optimism, no doubt, is the natural comfort I feel with the system myself. I told you to assume a personal bias in all economists unless there is proof of a truly saintly detachment. Personal bias makes me a reformer rather than a revolutionary. However, we cannot look usefully at the needed patching until we have seen what has happened to the market. On one point – it is hard to think of another – all economists of all faiths agree. The neo-classical system depends for its credibility and its workability on a credible, workable market. Could we talk about what has happened to the market ?

NICOLE: *Yes, but tomorrow. Because I want to know first how the neo-classical and Keynesian ideas differ from those of the socialists – Proudhon, Marx, Lenin. Why aren't these the alternative?*

JKG: Well, I've partly answered that question. I think the neo-classical or Keynesian system should be patched up instead, although that patching will not be small. The textbooks will have to go. So will the comfortable men and women who believe that a public office concerned with economics can be a haven of peace and rest, a place to commune with past truths. But let me get on to the socialists.

The ideas of the great socialists take us back again to the last century. And here there is a special problem. In this tradition,

Marx's ideas are central, even overpowering. They lend themselves to many interpretations, and his followers have been exceptionally free in making them. As I've said, American economists in high office reach into the future and adjust it to their needs; what they predict is what they need to have happen. In the Soviet Union and the other Communist countries, Marxists reach into the past and adjust Marx to *their* needs. Once, before his death in 1883, Marx looked at some of the interpretations to which his work had already been subject and declared that he himself was not a Marxist.

Marx held that the central tendency of the economic system is not to a benign equilibrium; it is to a destructive contradiction. Competition is a passing phase. As capitalism develops, large firms absorb the small ones, a process that Marx called capitalist concentration. Monopoly capitalism replaces the competitive market. By this process the firms, though large, become few and politically vulnerable. Meanwhile the workers are paid but a small part of the value they create. And in consequence of their industrial employment they become disciplined, aware of the exploitation to which they are subject and politically sophisticated – socialized, as Marx said. So at a certain point these two great forces – the attenuated capitalist power, its survival value gone the way of the dinosaur, and the disciplined, stronger, ever more potent force of the workers – meet. As the inevitable consequence, the capitalist power is overthrown; socialism, the workers' state, takes its place.

You ask if Marx is the alternative to the neo-classical system. In recent times, as the neo-classical system has seemed to be ever more remote from the reality and ever less able to deal with the modern crises of inflation and unemployment, there has been a tendency to think so. If Samuelson doesn't work, then surely it must be Marx. I've always regretted this, for it requires that Marx explain the world that exists a hundred years after his death. That is asking rather much. And, the obvious concentration apart, I don't believe that the development of capitalism has been along the lines that Marx predicted.

NICOLE: *Then is Marx obsolete too?*

JKG: Yes, I would say so. His ideas are, of course, as indelibly a part of our life and times as those of Adam Smith. And ideas affect action. But the development of the capitalist firm, which we must surely talk about later, has not been as Marx foresaw. It has taken power from the capitalist and given it to its own organization or bureaucracy, to what I have called the techno-structure. Partly in consequence, there has been a much less sharp confrontation with the workers than Marx thought would occur. Trade unions, on their part, have become much less revolutionary than he foresaw or would have wished. And unions and the modern welfare state have rubbed far more of the rough edges off capitalism than Marx ever imagined they could, although of this he did have some premonition where England was concerned. And, on the other side, the bureau-cratic and managerial problems of running a socialist economy have been far, far greater than Marx predicted. If economic performance in a socialist society had come as easily and with prospects as brilliant intellectually and otherwise as Marx took for granted (and Lenin also, before it became, for him, a matter of practical experience), there would be no capitalism left. No power or propaganda would have held people to capitalism.

NICOLE: *Now what about other ideas? I've read what you've written about such American economists as Thorstein Veblen. Is there hope there?*

JKG: In all countries – Germany, the United States, France, even Britain – there has always been a small group of econo-mists that lived outside both the Marxist and the neo-classical traditions. In Britain the most famous was J. A. Hobson, from whom Lenin drew a great many of his ideas. And, generally, the Fabians, the intellectual guide and conscience of the British Labour Party. All, however, were not in the respectable academic current of economic thought; my economic col-leagues had no difficulty giving George Bernard Shaw to the theater. In Germany in the last century Friedrich List was an enormously influential economist. He broke with the free-trade tradition of the classical economists and argued for tariff protection, a serious act of apostasy which, however, worked well for such new industrial countries as the United States or Germany, countries that were getting started in face of the more experienced British competition.

Another distinguished group of Germans – Roscher, Sombart, Schumacher (the father of E. F. Schumacher of *Small Is Beautiful*) and others – looked for economic truth in history. They may have found it, but their books were so vast that not many will ever know. In the United States there were economists who felt that the problems of a new country were different or who otherwise rejected the neo-classical orthodoxy. Henry George was one; he achieved world eminence in the last century for urging, in effect, the public ownership of all land. John R. Commons was another; Thorstein Veblen was a third. Commons, a greatly influential professor at the University of Wisconsin in the first half of this century, avoided theory and said that the test of economics was practical, useful reform. He concentrated on such things as devising a state income tax, compensation for the unemployed and better regulation of public utilities.

Veblen was, of course, the most important of all; his most famous work, *The Theory of the Leisure Class*, appeared just at the end of the last century, and he then went on to write *The Theory of Business Enterprise* and numerous other books of great originality and interest. Veblen's economic system turned onthe conflict which he believed to exist in modern economic society between the needs and imperatives of business and what could be done by engineers using the resources of the new science and technology, including the 'instinct to workmanship' of workers themselves. Engineers and workers could be immensely productive. Businessmen are impelled to keep this natural productivity under strict control in order to keep down production, keep up prices and make money out of what is produced. The idea had a certain vogue in the United States in the 1930s; it was called technocracy, and one Howard Scott was Veblen's prophet. It did not survive. I do not believe the conflict cited by Veblen exists, at least in the form he described. In any case, engineers need managers and organization if they are to be useful. Released from the bondage of the businessmen, they wouldn't produce more; they would most likely produce random products in a highly disorganized way at high cost.

Veblen, as Raymond Aron has said, was a greater sociologist than economist. His pleasure was in the mordant criticisms of the manners and pretenses of the affluent, and it is for this rather than for his economics that he is now read. Veblen had a considerable influence on my own manners and enjoyments. I don't believe that he ever wrote anything without reflecting with pleasure on the discomfort that it might cause the self-satisfied, the self-righteous and the rich, always assuming they would and could read it. Nothing gives me more pleasure than to look over something I've written and say, 'I don't think David Rockefeller will like that.' Sadness comes only when I realize that David probably won't bother to read it.

NICOLE: *Why, incidentally, do the Anglo-Saxons have such a great influence on economics, at least now?*

JKG: Natural arrogance, no doubt. But there are several better reasons. England was the great trading nation of the world in the eighteenth and particularly in the nineteenth centuries. And since trade – the market – is at the center of economics, it was natural that the British should be most studious and expert in the institution that was most nearly essential to their existence. The British were also the great innovators in central banking; the Bank of England, which dates from 1694, was the model for all the other central banks. Its leadership made the subject of money and banking, in its early form, a British discussion.

There's another reason which is little mentioned. We talked yesterday about whether economic policy was the same for all industrial countries. I said the important difference was between the poor countries and the rich. There is, however, one great difference between the rich nations. Some are much easier to manage than others. Britain is a difficult country to run, far more difficult than France or the United States. Nothing ever goes permanently wrong in France. It can suffer the most frightful misfortunes, as in 1870 when it was defeated and Paris was besieged, subject to revolution and partially destroyed, and again from 1914 to 1918 when the whole northeastern part of the country was lost with much damage, and yet again during the Occupation from 1940 to 1944. But then, sooner rather than later, it recovers and is more prosperous than ever before.

Britain, by contrast, leads a much more perilous existence. It depends more heavily on imports and exports. There must be enough of the latter to pay for the former, and movements in world prices and market demand can be upsetting and are beyond any British control. The British demand a far higher level of equity and fairness in the treatment of different income groups – unions, farmers, pensioners, civil servants – than do the French. So, at least until the North Sea oil arrived, British economic policy always had to be much more careful than that of France. For this reason it was the subject of much more detailed debate.

The United States is a much easier country to manage than Britain, and until recently many of our economic concerns were derivative – we discussed what the British were discussing. When I was young, it was assumed that anyone who really wanted to get his back into economics should go to England to study. You could get by in Cambridge, Massachusetts, but if you wanted to be in touch with the gods, you went to Cambridge, England.

NICOLE: *What about Austria? Didn't it produce famous economists?*

JKG: Yes. In the years between the wars, the 1920s in particular, many would have said that Austria was then pre-eminent. Joseph Schumpeter, Ludwig von Mises, Gottfried von Haberler, Friedrich von Hayek, Oskar Morgenstern, Fritz Machlup, were all together in Vienna at that time. All were devout and rigorous defenders of the neo-classical market, unrelenting opponents of all forms of government intervention, all strong evangelists for their beliefs. All, during the thirties and forties, transferred their ideas and their evangelism to the United States. The Austrian economy, which did badly while they were there, has performed brilliantly since they left. Some have seen this as cause and effect and spoken of Austria's revenge on America for her defeat in two wars. I doubt that this is true.

NICOLE: *But isn't Harvard the dominant place for economic discussion today?*

JKG: We certainly prefer to think so. However, the preoccupation at Harvard in recent times has been with rather narrow technical matters, the refinements to which I earlier adverted. Harvard economists have not taken much part in the recent debate over how to deal with inflation and unemployment. This keeps them out of controversy, leads to an atmosphere of contentment which, no doubt, makes for a happier family life. But the testimony of an older professor on these matters is deeply suspect; all of us are prisoners of nostalgia, given to evoking a golden age.

Some of Harvard's past esteem was also derivative; it came from being the conduit by which the Keynesian ideas reached the United States. It was Harvard economists – Alvin H. Hansen, Seymour E. Harris and a younger group among whom Paul A. Samuelson was the most influential – who made Keynes's ideas known on the American scene.

NICOLE: *And then these ideas passed over to the Roosevelt Administration and the New Deal, no?*

JKG: Yes, I have said many times that Keynes got to Washington by way of Harvard.

NICOLE: *Is it because of Anglo-Saxon predominance in economics that English is now the international language of business and trade?*

JKG: I'm not sure. Maybe the corporation is more responsible. Without everyone quite noticing it, English has become the lingua franca of modern business enterprise. As Philips and Renault extend their activities around the world, even though their origins are in Holland and France, their business is done in English. General de Gaulle would not be at all pleased.

NICOLE: *To get back to today, do you see the failure of the systems we talked about encouraging what we call the New Philosophers in France? Have these systems all failed the individual?*

JKG: I'm not, as you may judge, well read on the New Philosophers. They are, I gather, in retreat from Marxism and now deeply concerned with the relation of the economic system to the individual and vice versa. There is a conflict here which is inherent in all organization, capitalist or socialist. It is most acute in the modern socialist state. The conflict there is also greatly celebrated by, among others, those who most readily accept conformity in the non-socialist world. Marx, I might note, would be distressed by suppression of dissent anywhere, including in the socialist world. He was first expelled from Prussia for advocating and also practicing, among other inconvenient reforms, freedom of the press.

In every organization the individual yields some freedom to the purposes of the group. The question is how much and with what alternative. The modern great corporation imposes its own culture on its executives, creates its organization man. He adopts the ideas that serve or seem to serve the corporate purpose and offers them with resounding emphasis as his own. The corporation also imposes its own purposes, to the extent possible, on the consumer and on the state. So in modern capitalism too there is an inherent conflict between organization with its discipline and the individual.

The difference between the capitalist world and the socialist is that, in the former, one can, if one is so motivated and wishes to pay the price, contract out. That is what artists and intellectuals do. They don't turn up working for General Motors. General Motors, in contrast, is manned and led by people who accept, maybe like, the discipline or, in any case, appreciate the pay they receive for their surrender. I expect that many Russians are equally untroubled. Tolstoy said that most men like to give their lives over into the care of the regiment.

NICOLE: *You said that the failure of modern socialism was performance. Is that failure in relation to material achievement or in relation to the liberty of the individual?*

JKG: Both, no doubt. The failure in material performance was partly an accident of history. Perhaps it was the misfortune of socialism that it was first tried in Russia. Managing Russians may be even more difficult than managing Frenchmen. Also, in 1917, Russia was still a country of poor peasants and incompetent landlords, not of large, well-organized, capitalist enterprises. The other great socialist experiment has been in China. The Chinese are more gifted and experienced in organization than the Russians, but this is also a peasant land where, additionally, population presses heavily on resources. That kind of pressure means a low standard of living whether a country is socialist or non-socialist. So were one picking the last countries in the world in which to produce a socialist success, China and Russia would be prominent candidates, just after India.

Marx thought socialism should begin in Germany, and he was exceedingly prescient on this point. In the purely material sense, socialism in East Germany works very well. By some calculations, per capita Gross National Product in the GDR is now higher than in Britain. However, we saw the other day that the GNP is not a precise measure of happiness. With material success, freedom of expression and behavior take over as issues. It's why, I suppose, there still has to be the Wall.

Poverty restricts freedom without any help from the government; escape from poverty creates an inconvenient opportunity for thought.

In the western industrial countries, though alienation from organization is an issue, I think material performance is a more important one. Inflation, the resulting redistribution of income, the use of unemployment as a remedy for inflation, are our greatest sources of discontent. Also, the unequal development of the modern industrial system – its good performance in providing automobiles and alcohol and tobacco and cosmetics, its ghastly record on housing, medical care and the essential services of the great cities.

NICOLE: *Is a new system being born that draws on all of the old ones?*

JKG: Perhaps; it is sometimes hard to see what is before our eyes. The non-socialist economies are being forced increasingly into planning; energy is only the most dramatic case. They also have a growing public sector occupied by those industries such as housing, health care and mass transportation where the liberal system doesn't work very well. And there is another large and growing public sector or publicly aided sector – American railroads, British Leyland, Rolls-Royce, Lockheed, IRI in Italy – for the failed children of capitalism. At the same time, the socialist countries, we see, are making somewhat greater use of private initiative for small-scale activities. There is an important convergence here between the socialist and non-socialist systems – on similar large-scale organizations where these serve, on similar small-scale market structures where there is no alternative.

But the greatest change is in relation to the market. Once it was the regulator of economic activity; it is still so celebrated in the neo-classical orthodoxy. But it is in decline, and to replace it we are getting new bargaining relationships among the various claimants on income. These innovations are coming not in response to ideology but because the market system, as it decays, leaves us with a combination of inflation and unemployment which no one can defend.

NICOLE: *What specifically has happened to the market?*

JKG: It suffers from a peculiar form of affection. Everyone loves it except as it applies to himself or herself or to the organization to which he or she belongs. For the individual the market is a menace, an inconvenient and arbitrary force determining his income or price, which he seeks, and with increasing success, to influence or control. But I think we had better make that a separate subject of conversation.

Chapter 3
What Happened to the Market?

NICOLE: *Now can we discuss the market? Why does the neo-classical, liberal system place such emphasis on the market? And what is the market anyway?*

JKG: Originally, of course, it was a place where buyers and sellers actually came together and bought and sold food, cloth, clothing, cattle, intoxicants, other things of like reward. But now, by long custom, it is an abstraction; a reference to the market is to the general, continuing purchase and sale of some product or some service. There is no longer any geographical connotation. American corporation executives speak with pride of the tough life they encounter in the market-place. It's somewhere they've never been.

NICOLE: *So what conditions did the neo-classical economists believe necessary if the market was to work?*

JKG: The market, let me remind you, is the regulatory apparatus that takes the place of the state – of authority. If the market fails, so does the case against government intervention. Intervention becomes the alternative to anarchy or the exploitation of the weak by the strong. And to be an effective regulator, the market must be an impersonal force beyond manipulation by any individual or organization. One wouldn't want business firms – corporations – writing legislation by which they are themselves regulated. That is too agreeable for those so favored. Likewise one cannot have a regulatory mechanism in which the individual sets his own price. That also is too agreeable. Price-setting becomes impersonal, beyond the power of any participant, when there is competition. There should, in one of the oldest phrases in economics, be the competition of many sellers and many buyers. If any seller asks more than the market price, then all customers can go to those who sell at the market price. They are a readily available alternative. The presence or total withdrawal of any one seller or any one buyer doesn't appreciably alter the price in the market. So there is nothing any one buyer or seller can do to influence the market.

NICOLE: *Are these conditions ever really fulfilled?*

JKG: In the absence of government intervention, this kind of impersonal price-making does hold for such farm crops as cotton, wheat, feed grains or soybeans. If even the largest cotton producer dies, goes to heaven and takes his plantation with him, much as Howard Hughes, I now suspect, arranged to take his money with him, it will make no difference to the price of cotton. Big as he may be, he's unimportant in relation to the total production. So this is, indeed, an impersonally determined price which applies to all and which no single seller can influence or control. It's the kind of market which the neo-classical system assumed and in substantial measure still assumes. As a rough guess, around half of all economics lectures begin with the statement, 'Let's assume competition.'

NICOLE: *But it still seems to me the exception.*

JKG: It is – and increasingly so. And this is the vital point. In past times, when the classical ideas were taking form, the main items of commerce and the main products of agriculture and industry were food, fibers, cloth, fuel, lumber, elementary services. The producers of these things were numerous and small, and the resulting goods were also easily substitutable. The yarn from one mill or the cloth from one loom was much the same as that from another. So the competitive ideal was approximated. Applying the test, if one producer disappeared, the effect on price was not noticeable. But even then there were always exceptions. In classical and neo-classical economics there was always the flawing case of monopoly. This might be a natural monopoly – the man who owned a mineral springs with some unique peristaltic effect. He could charge those having difficulty whatever price brought the most profit; he didn't have to worry about someone coming along with the same product at a lower price. His price was personally, not impersonally, determined, and here obviously the market had a badly flawed regulatory effect. There was also the charter of monopoly. One of the easiest ways of doing someone a royal favor was to give him the exclusive right to sell some product. Playing cards were one of the many Elizabethan monopolies – an important though not exactly a basic industry. The *privileges* of the *Ancien Régime* were of the same sort – one of the many causes, as you learned, of the French Revolution.

Also, there was always a difference between the seller of a commodity and the seller of labor. The seller of cotton or cotton goods could wait until tomorrow or the next day or even next year if the price wasn't right. If a man selling his own labor postponed the sale, and particularly as workers were often more numerous than jobs, he most likely wouldn't eat that day. After a time this would become uncomfortable. So it was usually agreed that labor was sold in an inherently weaker market than goods. Liberal economists in the neo-classical tradition, though deeply opposed to monopoly, often looked upon the trade union with a somewhat favorable eye. It compensated for the peculiar weakness of the worker in selling his product. It was a semi-legitimate form of monopoly.

NICOLE: *What has been the effect of corporations and the government on the market? Has it been like that of the unions?*

JKG: Adverse, all three. Forty-odd years ago, when I was first studying economics, it was just coming to be recognized, and it's now accepted, that if instead of a single seller you have a small number – three, four, half a dozen, a dozen, twenty – selling the same product or service, you get roughly the same result as with only one. The notion of oligopoly – an exceedingly unmusical word – had come into economic discussion. It denotes several sellers rather than many or just one.

The reason is simple. If you have a small number of companies, as now in the automobile, chemical, pharmaceutical, rubber, steel, aluminum, electrical, computer or many other industries, each firm will see the common advantage in the most profitable price and the common disaster in price-cutting. So the resulting price will be much the same as with monopoly. The sense of the common or group interest allows firms, usually without any formal communication, to find the best price. This ability is not seriously disputed by economists; it is described in all the textbooks. It follows that if the economic system is taken over by large corporations, you no longer have an impersonal, competitive market. The individual firm has an important share of the total output. And its acceptance of the need to conform gives the industry an oligopolistic market in which there is power to set prices and for the group to regulate itself in its own interest.

NICOLE: *So neo-classical economics accepts the decline of the market?*

JKG: No. This is another vital point. It has accepted the fact of oligopoly, which is inescapable. But it has never made it the general case, and it has never accepted the consequences. Oligopoly is still regarded as an exception, an imperfection in the system. It is not supposed to impair, basically and generally, the operation of the market.

NICOLE: *But does it?*

JKG: Of course. In all the advanced industrial countries a relatively small number of corporations do a large share of all the business. In the United States a couple of hundred large industrial corporations now provide around 60 percent, not much less than two-thirds, of all manufacturing employment. Similarly the handful of big airlines, the two telephone companies, the three broadcasting networks, the separate power companies that are dominant in their respective industries and markets. Around fifty of the largest banks provide about half of all the banking services in the United States. The insurance business is yet more concentrated. Even retailing is dominated by a relatively small number of large chains. The overall result is that a couple of thousand big corporations now provide more than half of all private production of all goods and services. The modern economy breaks into two sectors, one consisting of a few very large firms and the other of a very large number – in the United States ten to twelve million – of very small firms. The small firms will not, I think, disappear. There are numerous functions for which the small firm headed by the owner works better. He has his own capital at risk, exploits himself and his family and is much more efficient. But in at least half of the economy the impersonal regulation of the market has given way to the partly or largely self-regulating power of the large corporation.

No one can say that if General Motors disappeared from the automobile industry, price and production would be unaffected. Or that if General Electric were to leave electrical goods or Du Pont chemicals, all would be much as before. I don't think anyone would argue that if IBM were to abandon the computer market, it wouldn't be missed. An inescapable consequence of the development of the large corporation is that price-making ceases to be competitive and impersonal. Instead, the corporation gains the essential power to make its own prices.

NICOLE: *But can't this be seen?*

JKG: A fair number of economists have managed to avoid the view. A very conservative group, dwindling in size I would judge, simply ignores the whole development. If you believe in the market, you don't allow such things to bother you; you deny that oligopoly makes any real difference. That is the position of Professor Milton Friedman and his very distinguished communicants. And, on occasion, they also produce statistics to show that concentration and oligopoly are no longer getting worse. Quite a few liberal economists accept that concentration and oligopoly undermine the neo-classical market but hold that the trend will somehow, someday, be reversed. Their faith is also in the competitive market. However, I must not exaggerate. An increasing number of economists concede the role of the large corporation. And there is more and more discussion of how to come to terms with it. It is the textbooks and the teaching that hold on to the impersonal rule of the market as though to life itself.

NICOLE: *Surely this isn't peculiar to the United States. Are you suggesting that this is an American misjudgement?*

JKG: I am an American but also, I trust, something of an observer of the general industrial scene. The development that I have just outlined is common to all the industrial countries. None is spared. It has not, I judge, gone quite as far in France as in Germany or the United States. But modern industry has everywhere the same basic dynamic.

NICOLE: *Certainly there is competition between big corporations. The automobile companies? Even oil?*

JKG: In advertising and model changes and gadgetry and other things that persuade the consumer. This is safe; it rarely, if ever, leads to price competition. The oil companies each try to sell more gasoline; they advertise the peculiar virtues of their own brand while knowing that it is interchangeable with all the others and may even have come from the same tank. But they don't cut prices. Anything that threatens the basic control over prices *is* banned. That is the real manifestation of market power.

NICOLE: *And the trade unions, you say, have countervailing power?*

JKG: Yes. Large corporations bring large numbers of workers together, and they are then rather easily organized. They see the power of the corporation in buying their labor so, as I suggested earlier, they have a very strong incentive to match that power in selling their labor. This I have called the tendency to the creation of countervailing power. So, as a nearly invariable rule, where one has large corporations controlling their prices, one has strong unions controlling the prices at which labor is sold. This, in turn, has a good deal to do with the modern problem of inflation.

NICOLE: *And government? How does that affect the market?*

JKG: As economies develop, more and more services are provided by the government – support to the weapons industry, education and the provision of qualified manpower, highways for the automobiles, research and development where, as in the case of nuclear energy or modern air transport, the costs or risks are too great for private firms, health services, housing, social insurance, transportation, rescue operations for private corporations that come on hard times, electricity and telephone services in many countries. All this we've seen. So the government in all countries, not only the socialist lands, becomes a very large producer of goods and provider of services. And much production for or by the government is outside the market. So the competitive market disappears in this part of the economy.

However, the government has a yet more important effect in modifying the market system. Where the market still works, where there is still competition, there is that mixed affection of which I spoke – the deep love for the market in principle, the great dislike for its punishment in practice. So the government steps in to mollify those who experience the practical effects, to ease the pain. It sets prices, or anyhow establishes minimum prices, for farmers. It sometimes establishes minimum margins for retailers to keep the competition there from being too harsh. Where, as occasionally happens, an oligopoly has difficulty maintaining prices, it comes to the government for help in doing so. We are now having such a rescue mission in the

United States for the steel industry. And our airlines have been fighting desperately to keep government price-fixing of air fares as well as control over the granting of routes. They naturally don't want any Freddie Lakers, to mention the most topical figure, getting loose in the domestic market. Government regulation of fares and route allocations, they have been arguing, is an exceptionally advanced form of free enterprise.

Finally, where workers do not have unions, the government establishes a substitute in the form of a minimum wage. One group of rather conservative economists in the United States accepts unions but is gravely critical of a legislated minimum wage. The distinction has always been something of a puzzle, for the minimum wage is the poor man's union; it serves the same function as a union for the poorest members of the working force. I never want to be unkind, but I strongly suspect my economic colleagues of defending competition and the market with most vigor where the people involved don't fight back.

So, to summarize, corporations, trade unions and the government have all united to impair or destroy the competitive or neo-classical market. Often it has been done with a sense of righteous purpose. Who would deny rescue to the poor farmer who would otherwise be ruined by the price of his wheat or cotton – or wine?

NICOLE: *But surely the government, especially in the United States, tries to preserve competition in the market. You just said that was the hope of liberal economists. What about your antitrust laws?*

JKG: The government tries. And some still hope. It's proof that hope does, indeed, spring eternal. The basic antitrust law in the United States – the Sherman Act – was passed in 1890, almost a hundred years ago. It was then greatly strengthened during the administration of Woodrow Wilson, when the Clayton and Federal Trade Commission Acts were passed. Since then it has been reinforced by yet further legislation. No effort has ever had such a fair and formidable trial. And, as we've seen, these laws have not checked the great thrust to concentration and oligopoly. King Canute looks down on those who administer our antitrust laws with the utmost understanding and sympathy.

NICOLE: *But you said liberal economists still have faith.*

JKG: These are laws designed to preserve the impersonal regulatory power of competition, ensure that there are many sellers and that monopoly and oligopoly are put down. Having seen the store that neo-classical economists set by the market, you will understand the resulting affection.

NICOLE: *What about the future? Can one think these laws could be made to work?*

JKG: We have never had an election in which liberal politicians did not promise to enforce the antitrust laws and in which the more reverent economists did not applaud the prospect. They both prefer hope to history. We've seen that these laws have had very little effect on the American development. Nor have they in my old home country, Canada, which has long had a Combines Act paralleling the antitrust laws of the United States. Or in Britain, which, since the Second World War, has had legislation, more cosmetic than real, against monopolies. It is persuasive that the development in the United States, Canada and Britain, which have had such legislation, has not been different from that in France, Germany, the Netherlands and Belgium, which have been too sophisticated or negligent to bother.

NICOLE: *The laws were not effective because nobody really wanted to enforce them or was it because the government wasn't strong enough to attack the power of the corporations?*

JKG: A little of both, but mostly because you can't drop a few stones into the river and stop the full force of the Mississippi. A truly vulgar American expression emphasizes the point: 'Just a fart in a windstorm.' There are some trends in social and economic affairs that are so massive and so powerful that legislation is inherently ineffective against them. This was true of the antitrust laws. The neo-classicists saw their relationship to an economic ideal; they did not see the impossibility of arresting as basic a tendency as the great development of the large modern corporation. Affection, as happens, clouded their vision.

I should add that some of the affection for our antitrust laws comes from their being an important industry, a significant source of income. Many of our best lawyers get their early legal experience in the government, enforcing, or trying to enforce, the antitrust laws. Then, when they need a larger house, their children are going off to school, their wives are tired of economizing or alimony has become a threat, they give up working for the Department of Justice and go on to defend the corporations against the antitrust laws. It's a very remunerative arrangement and gives lawyers a constructive stake in keeping the antitrust laws alive. The gross revenues from defending IBM alone were recently estimated in the *New York Times* at between ten and twenty million dollars annually, the cost of prosecuting being in addition. People come naturally to the defense of anything that sustains so lucrative a line of work.

NICOLE: *Are you saying that, in fact, no one really likes the market except the economists?*

JKG: Precisely. The market is an admirable vision which appeals greatly to economists with a secure income and tenure. But every person in real life seeks, above all, to get some control of his own income. It is, in fact, the most sought after and cherished of liberties. The most important and the most controllable dimension of a person's income is price or wage – the price at which he sells his product, the wage or salary at which he sells his services. Control – emancipation from the tyranny of the market – comes with control of one's price or wage.

NICOLE: *And how do you get such control? Remind me.*

JKG: The most obvious way is to be big in your market. Another is to have a union. Another is to get the government to protect you from the market with a minimum wage. Another is to have the government (or the European Economic Community) fix your minimum farm prices. Another is to be a high corporate executive; then you have the important power of being able to set your own compensation. This is accomplished in the large corporation by your appointing the board of directors that, among other ceremonial duties, sets your salary. Such a board is likely to be very cooperative. Executives who speak most warmly about the stern rule of the market usually have excellent control over the income that they get themselves.

It used to be taken for granted that the prices the Third World countries charged for their raw materials would be impersonally determined in world markets, and here, too, there has been change. OPEC reflects the discovery by producers of raw materials in general and oil in particular that they no longer need be subject to the tyranny of such impersonally determined prices. The example of the oil producers will not be lost on others, although their success may not be all that easy to duplicate.

So there is nothing that people try so hard to escape as the tyranny of the market price or wage. And one of the consequences of modern industrial organization and of democratic government responsive to the public voice is that more and more people are able to make this escape.

NICOLE: *Then why do economists adhere to the idea of the market so strenuously? That I don't see. I must really press you on this.*

JKG: I don't mind – much. It would be more surprising were economists to act otherwise. And it's why, for the true believers, we should react with sympathy. There is the enormous historic power of the market vision. Also, when something gets fixed in the textbooks, it becomes sacred writ. The textbooks respond to the accepted truth, thus to the salable truth and not necessarily to the real truth. There is also the fact that economists who have been abreast of the times have almost always found themselves in the minority; Alfred Marshall warned that nothing was so to be feared by economists as applause. And, without the market, the nature of the regulatory process in the economy is by no means clear. There is no sharply delineated theory complete with formulae and diagrams that one can teach.

What is certain is that, with the decline of the market, price-setting and other economic behavior pass out of the hands of the economist and into the realm of politics and the dynamics of corporate, trade union and other group behavior. So there is a strong even if unconscious impulse to hold on to the idea of the competitive and impersonal market in order to hold on to one's own subject matter. Again, there is nothing abnormal about this. I have heard that witch doctors hold on rather tenaciously to the concept of the witch.

NICOLE: *Is there any market system left or do we have instead the system of corporate, trade union or government price-fixing?*

JKG: Oh, yes, there is much left. I've learned, though with difficulty, that there is nothing for which one's critics so yearn as exaggeration; prove an overstatement and you seem to disprove the whole proposition. For many firms control over prices is imperfect. Many people have a little leverage on their income but not much. In either case, if the firm or person charges too much or performs badly, somebody else will come in and do the job cheaper or better. This isn't a serious threat in the automobile, chemical, telecommunications, computer, tire, weaponry, pharmaceutical or other large-scale industry or in most transportation. And the understanding on prices extends across international lines. If the Seven Sisters charge too much for oil, they need not fear that someone else will come in – oil fields, tankers, pipelines, refineries and all – and take their business away. But competition still works for the gasoline service station and the small trader and the restaurant and for a very large range of other small enterprises. Minimum levels of farm prices are now set in most countries. But here, too, there are limits; if these prices are too high, production will expand, surpluses will accumulate and governments will be restrained from raising the minimum levels. So the market still sets limits on government price action. And competition everywhere, including in the large-scale oligopolistic industries, regularly prevents a truly inferior product from being sold. The decline of the market is a highly irregular process, and this, indeed, is what helps the very faithful to say that it isn't happening at all.

However, no really big firm – none of the two thousand I mentioned – is without a good deal of power over its prices. In that half of the economy the neo-classical market is only a memory. In some new industries – computers, for example – it never existed. The market survives in the other half – among service enterprises, artistic enterprises (a growing part of the modern economy, by the way), among small retailers, small manufacturers, other small and owner-operated firms and, within limits, in agriculture.

NICOLE: *Don't small firms sometimes succeed? Polaroid, for example.*

JKG: Yes. Polaroid did; it became very large and remained independent. More often, though, the successful small firm, especially if it has some new product, gets taken over by a big one in the same business. The large firm can afford to pay handsomely to get control and be free of the worry and annoyance presented by its smaller competitor.

NICOLE: *What about the socialist countries – Poland, Yugoslavia, even the USSR and China? Don't they also make a certain use of the market?*

JKG: To some extent. There's a fascinating parallel here. In the western economies the orthodox don't want to admit that the market has declined. In the socialist economies the orthodox don't want to admit that the market is still necessary. But in Poland, Hungary, East Germany and especially in Yugoslavia there is general recognition that, for the repair of automobiles and appliances, the sale of gasoline, the operation of restaurants and other like enterprises, the market with its incentives is a very convenient way of organizing economic life. (In Poland agriculture is almost wholly subject to controlled market incentives.) In the non-socialist economies the orthodox are similarly reluctant to concede that the market gives way to planning in the industries which are dominated by large corporations.

NICOLE: *Now what does all this have to do with inflation and unemployment; how are these affected by large organizations and by what is left of the market?*

JKG: Have patience. But since inflation and unemployment are so important, maybe we should stop occasionally to see if we are making progress in understanding them. Obviously, if trade unions win power over the incomes of their members and corporations have power to set their prices, an increase in union wage scales can be passed on to the consumer in the form of higher prices. And you can be pleasant and generous with the boys on the shop floor if you don't have to pay them yourself and especially if you know that the increases will affect the other firms in the industry and that they, too, will respond, as the common interest requires, with higher prices. So you see at least the possibility of a wage/price spiral – wages bringing higher prices and higher prices bringing higher wages. If the market were still functional, unions couldn't raise wages; there wouldn't even be unions in the pure market condition. And if there were unions, employers would have to resist them. For prices being determined impersonally in the market and being beyond control, they couldn't be raised. So inflation is a plausible result of people escaping the market and getting control of their own prices and incomes. When industrial wages and prices rise, the government will also be under pressure to raise wages and the prices of the things that it sells or controls – postal services, railway services and air fares. Here too the market has gone. And farmers, you can bet, will be pressing for higher prices. If all of these prices go up, then we're going to have something that will look very much like inflation. So you see that the decline of the market bears rather directly on the prospect for inflation.

NICOLE: *And unemployment?*

JKG: We are making progress on this too. How, in the past, did governments keep prices from going up ? What was the lesson of Keynes ? It was that to prevent rising prices you tighten up on government spending, raise taxes, reduce private spending and have the central bank cut back on spending from borrowed funds. All this reduces the total or aggregate demand for goods and puts in reverse the methods by which the economy is expanded. This, in the United States at least, is still the ortho-dox anti-inflation therapy. But what is the first effect of such a reduction or restriction of demand ? If the market were still functioning, it would be on that impersonally set price. The price would fall. And when prices fall, inflation comes to an end, as President Coolidge would also have perceived. But now prices are controlled. That control is not affected by the reduc-tion in demand. If wages are shoving up prices, prices will still go up. The wage/price spiral will continue. So the first effect is that fewer goods get sold. And if sales fall off, then, of course, so do production and employment. If the price spiral continues then we have inflation and unemployment at the same time, as, unhappily, we do in real life today.

NICOLE: *That's not a very pleasant conclusion, is it?*

JKG: Not at all pleasant. Only when unemployment is very severe will unions be restrained from pressing for wage in-creases, and only when employers have considerable excess productive capacity will they be likely to resist wage increases. Until then there will be wage increases and price increases – inflation. And there will be unemployment. As we exempt our-selves from neo-classical orthodoxy, we see how unemploy-ment and inflation can be combined. But before we go further into that, I wonder if we shouldn't have a closer look at the corporation, national and multinational. We've seen how important it is.

NICOLE: *And money. Doesn't that have something to do with inflation?*

JKG: Yes. We'd better have a look at that, too.

Chapter 4

The Modern Large Corporation

NICOLE: *Most economists, I believe, talk about the firm as though there were only one kind. You have made a distinction between the economics which applies to the big company and that which applies to the small. Why?*

JKG: In neo-classical economics there is only one theory of the firm. This is assumed to embrace every kind of business and explain the behavior and impact of all – the smallest corner grocery store, the laundry, the massage parlor, General Mills, General Electric, General Dynamics, General Motors. As a participant in oligopoly, General Motors does have power in its markets. But its motivation and essential structure are thought to be the same as those of the automobile repair shop; it's a little outfit become large. This simplification goes back to the neo-classical commitment to the market. If sellers, like buyers, are numerous and competitive, they are likely to be small and operated by their owners or at most by the agents of the owners. And their concern, inevitably, will be in making as much money as possible; indeed, competition as pictured by neo-classical theory does not permit of any other goal. Were you to decide to be good and generous and easygoing, your costs would rise and rise some more. Soon you would be losing money, for the market returns only your costs plus the necessary minimum profit. If you raise your prices, all of your customers go elsewhere. If you don't, you continue to lose money, and presently you're out of business.

The economist's notion that there is only one kind of business firm was derived from the neo-classical view of the market, not from the reality of things.

NICOLE: *You don't agree?*

JKG: I certainly do not agree. And economists who are in touch with reality don't either. As the firm becomes very large, it changes in structure and motivation; it also has an accretion of power that extends far beyond prices. That there should be a difference between the small firm and the large is surely plausible. It requires an effort of will to believe that Exxon or General Motors or Nestlé or Citroën has the same basic characteristics as a grocer's shop, a small farm or a corner café. Nothing better disguises the reality of economic life than the assumption that there is a single theory of the firm.

NICOLE: *I want to get to the differences in a moment. But when did the companies start to get so big, and why?*

JKG: The corporation in its present form is a fairly recent development, pretty much of the last century. Until around a hundred and twenty-five years ago, corporations were regarded with considerable suspicion. The South Sea Bubble, the great English speculation in corporate charters and securities in the early eighteenth century, left a residue of suspicion of corporations in Britain. This, like so much else in economics, was carried over to the United States. The possibilities of abuse – fraud, monopoly, lassitude – were thought to outweigh the advantages. In France John Law's promotions – the issue of bank notes and the sale of vast quantities of securities to finance strictly hypothetical gold and silver mines in Louisiana – left a similar suspicion, although this was directed especially at banks. Corporations did exist – for trading (the English, Dutch and French East India Companies), for digging canals and later for building and operating the railroads. But each individual company was a special creation of the government and required a special act of Parliament or whatever. It was not until well along in the last century that general laws of incorporation were passed that allowed any person or any group to charter a corporation as a basic human right.

Then, as industrial production increased in scale – iron and steel, artillery and ordnance, petroleum and kerosene, shipping and shipbuilding, chemicals – corporations grew in size. This was to accommodate the larger scale of industrial activity and realize the efficiencies of large-scale production. The last quarter of the last century was a time of great corporate growth in the United States, Britain, Germany, France. And the trend to greater size has continued. If you're going to make automobiles in large numbers, recover oil from under the North Sea, build a pipeline across Alaska to the North Slope, there must be an enterprise of considerable size – there's no escape from that. The mass-consumption society has its counterpart in the mass-production society.

NICOLE: *There must be other reasons. Big firms also diversify, produce many different things.*

JKG: Sure. Large tasks, the economies of large-scale production, do not explain why the International Telephone and Telegraph Company is big not only in telecommunications but in electronics and in hotels, in fire insurance, in revolutions and, until lately, in the renting of automobiles. The imperatives and efficiencies of large-scale production do not explain the modern conglomerate with its operations in totally unrelated fields of activity. They don't even explain why General Motors should have more or less autonomous divisions making Cadillacs, Buicks, Oldsmobiles, Pontiacs and Chevrolets. Each of these could be a separate company. Indeed, for reasons of efficiency as well as consumer persuasion, GM has to break up its operations into these smaller, more manageable units.

The further reasons for great size begin with the urge to empire building – the Napoleonic complex brought to business. Business, like the older aristocracy, has its order of precedence. Honor and obeisance go naturally to the head of the biggest firm. So do the best pay and the better private jets. The head of General Motors sits on the dais, the small clothing man watches the proceedings from the next room on closed-circuit television. So everyone tries to become big or bigger.

Growth also rewards the people in the firm who bring it about. The engineer who designs a new piece of suburban gadgetry – a lawn-mower that can be guided by transcendental meditation – and the marketing man who designs a new way of selling some old gadget find themselves in charge of the resulting enlarged operation within the firm; then they have more subordinates, more responsibility, more prestige and more pay. So in the modern corporation there are many people who are seeking to expand sales. This becomes the ethic of the enterprise, and it's one reason why the modern corporation measures its overall success extensively by its rate of growth.

Finally, and most important of all, the larger the corporation the more power it has – the more power over prices, as we've seen, and also over its costs, the government and, ultimately, its earnings. And from its earnings comes its own supply of capital for investment – a most important advantage over the small firm. The bigger it is, the better it can minimize risk and plan operations and investment with assurance as to the outcome.

NICOLE: *I understand about prices. Could you be more specific on these other powers? Could we go over this more fully?*

JKG: Oh, by all means. The control of prices is, of course, the most obvious power. This allows the basic escape from the tyranny of the market for which all people and organizations so greatly yearn. But a large oil company, unlike a small distributor or refiner, can also reach back to the oil fields at home or in some distant desert to assure its supply of crude. A big steel company can reach back and control its supply of iron ore. A large retail firm such as our Sears, Roebuck can organize manufacture of its own appliances. Such action, too, minimizes the uncertainties of the market. Small manufacturers are much more at the mercy of the market in buying raw materials, small retailers in buying goods for resale. All small businessmen are much more vulnerable to suppliers, who can hold them up on prices or cut off supply.

Large size also gives greater access to the consumer. If you turn on the television in the United States, you learn immediately, since you are a woman, of the need for keeping your skin moist, otherwise pliable and even clean. Were you a man, you would hear of the facial disfigurement and resulting social ostracism from the use of an inadequate razor. You must be careful about your skin, Nicole, when you visit New York. We take it very seriously. And, woman or man, you see on television the shape of the automobile that is most nearly consistent with nirvana, the beer which is most nearly coordinate with beatitude, good fellowship, zest for life and a decently small stomach. By such means, the corporation reduces uncertainty as to whether its products will be sold. As it wins power over prices, it wins power over sales. But with television advertising costing many thousands of dollars a minute, this power is only available to corporations that are large enough to afford the price.

Then there is power in the government. The small firm by itself has only the influence of the citizen in general. There is no way the individual small businessman can bring power effectively to bear for his own special needs. He can unite with others, as do farmers, to pursue a common purpose. But this requires agreement on that purpose. And money must be collected to pay the cost. The head of a large corporation has an automatic entrée to the highest offices in the government. When the heads of the big New York banks arrive in Washington to tell of some needed modification of the free enterprise system, the word goes out, as Hubert Humphrey once said: 'Open wide the gates, the gods are coming through.' There is no similar ceremony for a little savings-and-loan man from Dubuque. (Dubuque, I believe, is very much like Tours in France.) The big firm can pay for its own lobbyists – lawyer-statesmen, they would prefer – in Washington, and I imagine the same is also true in Paris. There is a more subjective, but perhaps more important, power from being big. The large corporation has a sizeable, articulate and influential group of people who run it; they easily persuade themselves that whatever their firm needs in Washington is sound public policy. And news-papers, television commentators and the radio often reflect their views, for they are the most vocal and eminently respectable part of the community. No one ever got a reputation for radicalism by agreeing with Chase Manhattan. I've said many times that in the modern industrial community the voice of the affluent, which includes, notably, the voice of corporate management, being so articulate, is regularly heard as the voice of the masses.

Finally, a large corporation can conduct its own foreign policy. The big multinational oil companies have their own policy in dealing with the Middle Eastern governments. Sometimes it differs from that of the State Department. If it is the same, it is partly because these firms have a good deal of influence on the State Department. The Lockheed Corporation, in conducting its foreign policy in Japan, Holland, Italy and elsewhere, has had more success in destabilizing governments than has the CIA, with the difference that Lockheed operated only against friendly governments. Japanese cabinet ministers and Dutch princes aren't vulnerable to the influence or financial resources of the average retail grocer.

NICOLE: *In France we think of the large corporation as having power from its ability to offer or withdraw employment. If it threatens a shutdown, the government quickly pays attention.*

JKG: This too is a source of influence. It's what saves the firm that is in financial trouble. With us it is also very important where weapons orders are concerned. A firm that might otherwise close down has special leverage in getting orders from the Pentagon. And with the Congress.

You asked me earlier about how political economy became economics. You can see how the big corporations are now putting a significant political element back into economics.

NICOLE: *Does that mean that the textbooks should have a section on corporate political influence? Or corporate bribery?*

JKG: In the advanced courses it would be called econometric

aspects of extra-legal cost functions. It is partly because economics cannot digest the political operations of the corporation in such a refined way that these things are ignored in the textbooks. Not many economists live so far out of the world that they would deny the political power of the modern corporation, its importance in real life. But there is no elegant theory of corporate thimble-rigging and political subornation which lends itself to university instruction. So it has to be ignored. I must, as you see, come to the defense of my professional friends whenever possible.

NICOLE: *Is the military-industrial complex another aspect of that power?*

JKG: This, of course, is the closest relationship between the corporation and the state. A symbiosis. The United States Air Force lets the big weapons firms know of the weapons systems – planes, missiles, guidance apparatus – it would like to have. With equal pleasure, the weapons firms design and produce the things the Air Force wants. A perfect relationship and a model for any marriage.

There is also an extensive exchange of people between the Pentagon and the management of these weapons firms. Executives of the big weapons manufacturers often move into senior procurement posts in the Pentagon for a tour of duty. When admirals or generals retire, they frequently become vice-presidents of one or another of the big weapons firms. This interchange gives an intimacy to the relationship between the corporation and the government, and this also is available only to the large enterprise. Once, some years ago, a Marine general who was a friend of mine opened a small hotel in Vermont. He went broke very soon afterward. No one ever went broke as a vice-president of General Dynamics.

NICOLE: *So it is the producer and no longer the consumer who holds economic power in this system.*

JKG: In substantial measure where the big firm is involved.

But again one must avoid exaggeration. The textbooks speak of the sovereignty of the consumer, which is, of course, hyperbole; it has declined along with the market. However, it would be as wrong to speak of producer sovereignty. The producer influences the consumer but also within limits. One cannot yet sell the consumer an automobile, no matter how beautiful and with whatever persuasion, unless it has an engine and even a steering wheel. However, we do have an indirect measure of producer power in the rise of what is called consumerism. Any exercise of power begets a reaction from those subject to it. If producers hadn't taken power, consumers wouldn't be reacting.

NICOLE: *Is there any limit to the size of a corporation? Can it become larger and larger – endlessly large?*

JKG: There is no clear upper limit. No one fifty years ago would have imagined that corporations could be as big as they are now. And by dividing the corporation up into separate units for administration, it does seem possible that the inefficiencies of large scale can be avoided. Or they are less than the advantages which large size confers in greater market, public and social power.

NICOLE: *You invented the word 'technostructure'. What do you mean by that?*

JKG: I said a moment ago that the structure of the very large firm is different from that of the firm in the textbooks. The technostructure highlights the difference. In the large corporation, decisions on all important matters are taken not by one person but by many. A decision to develop or launch a new product, open a new plant, operate in a new country, draws on many different branches of knowledge and experience. No one person has it all, so the decision requires the combined judgement of the production men, marketing savants, engineers, scientists, lawyers, accountants, labor-relations experts and other custodians of specialized knowledge. Each participant contributes a small slice of that specialized knowledge. All who so participate are the technostructure. The term has achieved general currency, and I couldn't be more delighted. Partly it is because some of the most respected economists said it wouldn't fly, and I have the usual mean pleasure in such error, my attempted fine character notwithstanding. But, also, people only adopt a word for general use if it is needed, if it describes something for which hitherto there was no good designation.

As the firm grows larger, the technostructure becomes the effective governing power for reasons that are not mysterious. Unless you have the knowledge that allows you to participate in making decisions and do participate, you can't be influential.

NICOLE: *You have said that the big corporation takes power away from its owners, from the capitalists, and partly socializes it.*

JKG: Yes. But the point is not original with me. The tendency has long been recognized, although again it has never been fully integrated into neo-classical thought. In the early 1930s, two brilliantly original scholars, Gardiner Means and the late Adolf Berle, both of Columbia University, looked into the management of the two hundred largest American corporations. They found that around half were controlled by their management – which is to say, the management appointed the board of directors which then appointed the management. A kind of closed-circuit system of self-approval. Since then the power of the technostructure has continued to increase, perhaps at an increasing rate.

As I just noted, as the corporation gets larger, its decisions become more complex. That reduces the power of uninformed outsiders and particularly of the stockholders. And as it gets older and larger, its stock becomes more and more dispersed. Inheritance taxes, philanthropy, prodigality, alimony and general taxation all act to distribute it among more and more people and institutions. Not long ago Professor R. J. Larner went back to the two hundred largest corporations in 1963 and found that, by then, in nearly 85 percent there was no stockholder or group of stockholders that owned as much as 10 per cent of the stock. In the very largest, no individual or group owned as much as 1 percent. Such minimal ownership, of course, gives no power. But the matter of participation, with its associated information, is even more important for exercising influence. No owner, large or small, who isn't part of the technostructure has access to the information that allows of useful judgement on decisions. No person who isn't intimately involved with the everyday exchange of information in General Motors can be useful on a decision on a major new automobile design or whether to open a plant in Singapore or Taiwan. No stockholder in Shell can say anything helpful on tactics for dealing with the Arab states, especially since most of those dealings are not even revealed to any stockholder, at least until they are completed.

NICOLE: *What about the board of directors? Surely it represents the stockholders, the owners.*

JKG: The board of directors in the large corporations, as I've just said, is appointed by the management. That tells something of its independence. But in most cases it is largely decorative, so far as aged males are ever decorative. It meets once every two months for a few hours. If the decisions are important, they are complex. Those directors who are not members of management – of the technostructure – know little about the decisions they are taking. No serious business executive can argue otherwise. To do so is to confess that running a modern corporation is a simple-minded exercise that does not require serious knowledge and attention.

In fact, the directors of the modern large corporation are treated with ceremony and respect and allowed to ratify decisions that have already been taken. Giving people the impression of power when, in fact, they have none is an old art form, one that is practiced with great finesse not only in the corporation but at high political levels in Washington and, I suspect, also in Paris. I've seen it operate at the White House.

You work out the proper course of action with those who are responsible and informed and do so with the greatest care. Then you ask the President to make a decision. After some discussion, he does, and he makes the decision you want because you avoid giving him any plausible alternative. Then you stand by and smile in approval and admiration when he goes out to announce it to the press.

NICOLE: *If the owners or their representatives have no real power, it doesn't make much difference who owns the corporation.*

JKG: Not really.

NICOLE: *Nationalization, which is such an important subject with us, makes no great difference then?*

JKG: For the very large firm it certainly makes less difference than most people imagine. The truly giant corporations – and, as I said earlier, they account for more than half the production of the modern industrial economies – are independent republics of their own management. As it is difficult for the stockholder to have information that affects decisions, so it is difficult for taxpayers to have information that allows of influence. And as the board of directors, for the same reason, is denied real power, so also the legislature. Just as uninformed intrusion by the stockholder would be damaging, so uninformed intrusion by a legislator or other public official is damaging.

Of course there are some differences. Where the stock of a corporation is owned by the government, there is likely to be more public knowledge of its operations. Management cannot so easily assert that something is the proprietary information of a private business. There is also, one imagines, somewhat more concern for public and legislative opinion. But the differences – as Renault, Rolls-Royce, the Tennessee Valley Authority all show – are not that great.

NICOLE: *Why, then, do executives resist nationalization?*

JKG: In all countries corporate executives strongly affirm the sanctity and prerogatives of private ownership while removing from that ownership all the reality of power. It's the liturgical aspect of economic life. No business convention ends without the ritual hymn of praise for rugged individualism and private enterprise even though the individualism is now manifested by good, conformist organization men who themselves have liquidated the power of the old capitalist free-enterprisers. You should be glad that economics has its romance too.

Also, I suppose, executives resist public ownership because, like most of us, they fear the unknown.

NICOLE: *I've read that American women own more than half of all common stocks traded on the New York Stock Exchange and so are the controlling voice in American industry. How do you reconcile that with what you've just said?*

JKG: Some men believe some women will believe anything. Or maybe the men believe it themselves. Have you ever heard of an angry band of women taking over a corporation, firing the management and putting themselves in charge? I might note that above the $25,000 pay range, employment in American corporations is 97 to 98 percent male – or was three or four years back when I looked up the figures. If women are in control, they are being sexist in a remarkably perverse way.

NICOLE: *If the technostructure excludes the owners, can it let the workers in? In Europe there is great talk of putting representatives of workers on boards of directors.*

JKG: It's called codetermination, and I'm not wildly enthusiastic about it. It puts worker representatives on boards that have no real power now. So what has been accomplished? Also, if the workers on the board flex their muscles and insist on intervening, it could be the same uninformed intrusion that is bad when it comes from stockholders or politicians. I've always believed more is to be gained from direct trade union bargaining – a rather traditional American view.

However, maybe the American view is not completely applicable in Europe. Our boards of directors are more purely cere-monial than those of some European corporations. Some European boards are smaller and more directly involved with management. And the Germans appear to have found codeter-mination useful, at least in a cosmetic way. Maybe one should keep an open mind. I do notice that American, British and French conservatives who talk about the great post-war success of Germany never mention the inclusion of union representa-tives on the boards of directors as a reason. I wonder why?

NICOLE: *You would apply the same principle to consumer, minority and similar representatives?*

JKG: Yes – again in the American context. A few years ago there was a move in the Harvard faculty to have the univer-sity's shares in the big corporations voted in favor of represen-tatives of the public rather than automatically for the directors whom the management had selected. I supported the effort because of the grief it caused the Harvard treasurer, a goodly man of presumed financial competence, unquestioned instinct for conformity and breathtaking respectability in the Boston banking world. I found it an agreeable form of sadism. I never imagined that those votes would accomplish anything.

Of late, some American corporations have actually been looking for black, Spanish-speaking nuns to put on their boards of directors. They've learned that such window dres-sing doesn't hurt a bit.

NICOLE: *You say this loss of power by the stockholders is not accepted by economists, is not fully integrated into the subject?*

JKG: The fact is not seriously disputed. But the consequences have never been fully worked into either the neo-classical or Marxian systems.

NICOLE: *Why not?*

JKG: Both neo-classicists and Marxists need the capitalist. The neo-classical firm must be run by an owner-entrepreneur who has no thought but to maximize earnings. The technostructure introduces some very tedious complications. Maybe it *does* want to maximize its own earnings. But quite plausibly, since this brings prestige, power and also pay, it could be more interested in growth – the empire building that I mentioned. And different corporations could have different goals. As always, if reality is too inconvenient, you tend to ignore it. The Marxists also need the capitalist. He is the economic, political and social pivot of their system, the ogre they are taught to fear and hate. They cannot have him losing power to the professional managers.

NICOLE: *We always come back to inflation and unemployment. Does the rise of the technostructure have an effect on them?*

JKG: On inflation certainly. The old-fashioned capitalist fought the trade unions not only out of pleasure and conviction but because it was his money that was involved. When the technostructure faces the union, it is acting on behalf of stockholders it doesn't know and whom, short of supreme foolishness, it no longer has reason to fear. As between having to pay yourself and not having to pay yourself, there is, in economics as elsewhere, a noteworthy difference. But also, as we've seen, the technostructure doesn't really need to sacrifice the interest of the stockholders in wage negotiations. Since it can control or influence its own prices, it can pass increased costs on to the public. This is ordinarily better than having a long and also very costly strike. Much of the anger and acerbity has gone out of labor relations in modern times. The rise of the technostructure is assuredly one cause.

NICOLE: *Could we continue with this next time? Doesn't the multinational corporation present special problems?*

JKG: As to your first question, surely. As to your second, I am less certain than most people.

Chapter 5

Nationalization
and Multinationalism

NICOLE: *In France nationalization of the large corporations is the most urgent subject of political discussion and the source of the big dispute on the left. Could I press you further on this? Why is nationalization less discussed in the United States?*

JKG: A different trade union tradition, in part. The early socialist tendencies in the American trade union movement, those of the IWW – the International Workers of the World – provoked a furious reaction and were pretty severely defeated. Samuel Gompers and the American Federation of Labor then came along in the early part of this century with the idea of business unionism – unionism that was without political aims, concerned only with higher wages and better working conditions and that wholly accepted the system. In the thirties and forties there was a Communist-dominated movement in part of the CIO – in the new industrial unions. It came under heavy and effective attack from the AFL and the more conservative unions within the CIO itself. Those battles pretty well took care of socialism in the American labor movement.

But socialism has encountered other difficulties. The Establishment in the United States has been more successful than its European counterpart in equating it with original sin. Americans have also been more successful in disguising the socialism we have. And a passion for socialism requires a greater sense of discomfort and injustice than most of my countrymen possess. That's another way of saying that for a good many

Americans the system either seems good enough or seems capable of being so reformed that it will be good enough.

NICOLE: *Where do you stand?*

JKG: Looking just at public ownership, I've always thought there was a powerful case for nationalizing our big weapons firms. They get their business from the government, operate on and with capital provided extensively by the government. Only their profits are in the private sector. If they were publicly owned, they could then no longer operate behind the fiction that they are private enterprise and exempt in most respects from public scrutiny. So they would be more clearly accountable for what they do. They would be more restrained in their lobbying. Salaries and bribery, foreign and domestic, would be under closer watch. There would be more to fear from the General Accounting Office, the Congress and the *Washington Post*.

NICOLE: *Would there be fewer weapons?*

JKG: I'm not sure about that. It's not certain that the Pentagon is entirely under the control of the government or the people of the United States. It has its own independent military policy. But at least the whole situation would be visible. If there were lobbying for a new bomber – some new flying dinosaur justified only by the earnings it returns, the B-1 being our most recent example – it would be done more or less exclusively by public employees. That would require more caution.

I also accept, as do most Americans, the need for socializing necessary production or services that do badly in private hands. The only difference here is that I don't try to be tactful about it. Railroads are a case in point. There is no country in the world where private enterprise is wholly successful in running a good railroad. And yet railroads are still necessary. So the state must step in. In the United States we've recently nationalized the north-eastern railroads with the elaborate pretense that the resulting company is still strictly a private enterprise.

I see no reason for such circumlocution even to spare the sensitive feelings of my conservative friends.

In the United States we also acknowledge the need for socialism or government intervention for the failing large corporation, something I mentioned earlier. Our free-enterprisers convert to socialism, as do Frenchmen or Englishmen, when government is the only solution for survival.

In France you take for granted that electricity gas and telecommunications should be publicly owned. That is my instinct, and we in the United States also have a good deal of public ownership, especially in electricity supply. But I regard this as a practical matter to be tested by results. I don't think Americans are deeply dissatisfied with the service they get from their private telephone companies. It's expensive, but it works. A few years ago a somewhat indiscreet professor from Czechoslovakia visited me in Cambridge. He had been doing some phoning and was rather amusing about it. 'You know, if our telephone calls went through as well as yours do, we'd make a great case for the advantages of socialism.'

We also accept a great deal of socialism in the housing industry and have a government department of sorts to administer it. There is no country where capitalism builds acceptable houses for people of middle income and the poor, and the United States is no exception. Housing, I might add, fails because it has never developed large and competent business units with an effective and competent technostructure.

Like other Americans, I accept government intervention in the health industry. Once this was called socialized medicine, and the term was thought pejorative. Then it became evident that people, worrying about the costs of private medical care, were coming to think well of socialism in this area. Opponents of a national health system had to drop the reference.

Our practice on public ownership is not so different from that of Europe. Mostly it's a matter of terminology. With you, socialism is an evocative word; with us, medicine possibly apart, it is not. So, where it is necessary, we find a euphemism.

We take over railroads, insure bank deposits or bail out the Lockheed Corporation not as a form of socialism but to protect and promote private enterprise.

NICOLE: *Does the technostructure have a similar existence in both public and private corporations?*

JKG: Oh, yes. And in both it requires independence. As I've said, the technostructure cannot suffer the uninformed intrusion of either stockholders or politicians; if it does, the quality of the decisions will be adversely affected.

NICOLE: *In the nationalized enterprise, what is the proper relationship between the firm and the state? How do you protect operational autonomy and still ensure response to public need? Aren't they sometimes in conflict?*

JKG: The problem of modern socialism is not a shortage of faith but a shortage of performance. As I said before, if socialism worked easily and successfully, the world would now be socialist. In the proper relationship there must be clear objectives and then there must be the maximum freedom for the enterprise in pursuing those objectives. There must still be a supervisory body representing the government, but its functions must be confined to seeing that the rules are observed and the objectives achieved. I once suggested that the nationalized firm should have not a board of directors but a board of public auditors. This would be appointed by the government and be composed of men and women of great integrity and high professional competence. They would not interfere with management, but they would have access to all information on the operations of the enterprise. Were there any breach of the rules, they would have power to take corrective action, including the right to discharge those responsible.

The rules would reflect the broad public purpose – no gross misleading of consumers, no mistreatment of particular categories of workers, no bribery or other malfeasance at home or abroad, respect otherwise for the law. Within this framework the management would have autonomy of decision. And the test of its performance would be its ability to sustain a satisfactory rate of earnings and growth. There happens to be no other test of efficiency, and certainly none which is sufficiently clear and objective. The public firm, like the private firm, should submit its targets for earnings and expansion and be held responsible for results. And, I repeat, for the public firm as for the private one there must be full freedom of decision as to how to achieve those results.

NICOLE: *Would you make the public firm responsible for providing jobs, keeping up employment?*

JKG: No. There are a few industries, railroads being almost everywhere an example, that must be run at a loss. But no firm should be asked to take losses in order to provide employment. That is the fatal temptation to which all socialist governments are prey. It means that manpower and plant and executive skills are being wasted on products that people don't think worth the price. It has a demoralizing effect on the enterprise and, needless to say, it's the public that must pay for the loss. Also, nothing gives conservatives so much joy as a publicly owned firm that survives only with large subsidies.

NICOLE: *If the public enterprise must be run at a profit by a technostructure that must be independent, doesn't that narrow the difference between the public and private corporation still more?*

JKG: Yes.

NICOLE: *But surely if profits are made, they would go to the government?*

JKG: Agreed. And this is another reason why earnings should remain the test of the performance of the publicly owned enterprise. Governments are generally in need of revenue.

NICOLE: *Are we making too much of the issue in France?*

JKG: Maybe. But I welcome the discussion. And public ownership, even if no great change is involved, is a natural next step. No one can believe that the modern private corporation, a republic as I said of its own management, is the perfect achievement of man and God. I take that back; there may be quite a few who believe it.

NICOLE: *In France it is being argued that socialist objectives can be achieved if the government has a controlling interest in a corporation, a majority of the voting shares. Is the difference between majority and full ownership important?*

JKG: This isn't a matter to which I've given much thought. My instinct is to think it doesn't make much difference. In either case there is power to set the rules and inform the public. In both, management must have a clear mandate to increase sales, make money and have the autonomy that allows it so to perform.

NICOLE: *Now can we talk about the multinational corporation? What's special about it?*

JKG: The amount of speechmaking it provokes. When I'm invited to give a lecture outside the United States, I almost never ask what topic would be preferred. I know the answer: 'Professor, we would like to have you talk about the multinational corporation.' I know several scholars who make a very decent living going around the world telling of the dangers of the multinational corporation, the threat it poses for civilized existence. The best-paying audiences, they tell me, are the executives of multinational corporations themselves. It is genuinely exciting for them to learn how dangerous they are.

I have a more relaxed view. The multinational enterprise is mostly an accommodation to the needs of modern international trade. A hundred years ago most such trade was in wheat, rice, cotton, copper, coal, iron, other simple products, and for it there was no need for any communication between the producer and the consumer. The producer could load the stuff on a ship or consign it to an exporter who did. From there it went on to the importer or the ultimate user in the receiving country. The user might not even know in what country the wheat was grown.

Things are very different with automobiles, machine tools, computers, television sets. The firms that produce these things must have organizations in the receiving country to assemble them, to market them and, on occasion, even to repair them. A large-frame computer cannot operate more than a couple of weeks without attention from the firm that built it. So, with modern international trade, firms must go abroad with their products. They become multinational as a matter of course.

There is another reason they must export themselves along with the goods. Volkswagen, Volvo or Renault, when it sells automobiles in the United States, needs someone there to persuade the United States government that its cars meet emission and safety standards. And it may need modifications or adjustments in those standards. That, too, requires a presence. Soon it will also seem economical, as it has to Volkswagen, to do some manufacturing in the receiving country as well. No such considerations entered the thinking of the wheat grower or the coal miner. International trade in things like automobiles and computers means automatically that there will be multinational corporations.

NICOLE: *Oil isn't a manufactured product; it comes from the ground.*

JKG: I hoped you wouldn't think of that. Of course there are other incentives to multinationalism. As I said earlier, the large corporation reaches back to get control of its raw materials, something which takes it into other countries. This is the case with the oil companies. And there is also empire building. When a management has exhausted the market possibilities of Holland or Belgium or Luxembourg, it begins, naturally, to look abroad. Who wants to be big in Luxembourg when he can be big in the world? Even Americans are susceptible, self-effacing and modest though we are. In the mind of every business executive lurks the thought of global reach and global power; of dismounting in Paris from his own jet or maybe just the Concorde; of having someone say, 'Sir, may I take care of your passport?'; of being greeted by a row of obeisant and admiring housecarls; and of gazing on some new and uniquely hideous offense to the Paris skyline and saying, 'That is mine.'

NICOLE: *But isn't part of the attraction to multinationalism the ability to produce in countries where labor is cheap?*

JKG: Yes, the multinational corporation goes abroad to produce with cheap or more efficient labor. That explains some of the modern development of Singapore, Taiwan, Hong Kong. Workers new to the industrial system almost always work harder than those in the older countries, who are accomplished in the art of bunging off. They compare life and pay on the assembly line with the worse life and pay on some ghastly farm. And along with lower wage costs go fewer regulations and lower levies for social insurance and public services. However, I do not consider the search for cheap labor to be the major impulse to multinational development. Labor that is cheap is, in many countries, also inexperienced, unreliable or otherwise undisciplined. The socialization of the labor force that Marx described at first increases its efficiency. If lower wages were a decisive factor, all production would now be in India. Low wages as a cause of multinationalism owe a lot to the celebration they receive from the trade unions.

NICOLE: *Have multinational corporations become threats to the sovereignty of governments?*

JKG: Yes. But all corporations are. That is the real, important and almost completely neglected point. We have seen that the modern large corporation needs a great many things from the government, and gets them. In getting them, it invades the sovereignty of the government. The large national corporation makes just as heavy an assault on national sovereignty as the large multinational firm does. The large American firm accommodates Washington to its needs. The large French firm persuades the French government in the same way. And so it is in Britain, Germany, Sweden or wherever. The multinational corporation, when it comes into a country, also persuades the host government as to its needs. It may establish a lobby, work on legislators, influence public opinion. Only because it is a foreign corporation does this look more serious than the similar invasion of sovereignty by a national corporation. I doubt that it is ever more serious; on occasion it may be more tactful and cautious.

When I was a youngster in Canada, to cite my favorite example, it was assumed that the Canadian Pacific Railway, then a very large and powerful organization, would get what it wanted from Ottawa. Its dignity required that it instruct, not ask. I can tell you that my neighbors who were farmers didn't much like the freight rates that this invasion of sovereignty produced. I very much doubt that General Motors, General Electric, Ford, and Du Pont, as they operate in Canada, have ever been so ruthless. But, being multinationals, their power is much more celebrated. Even given the great sophistication of the French people, I wonder if it isn't easier to get attention for the intrusions of the Ford Motor Company on French culture and sovereignty than for those of Citroën or Peugeot.

NICOLE: *Maybe. But doesn't the multinational have a strong bargaining position from its ability to bring in or withdraw capital and employment?*

JKG: To some extent. But it's a two-edged sword. Nothing puts a multinational corporation in such bad odor as the use of this threat. It's a great way to lose friends. Even if the Ford Motor Company threatens to leave England, as it did not long ago, it will still want to sell automobiles in England. And, of course, it can only leave once.

NICOLE: *Doesn't the multinational contribute to protectionist attitudes? Because of this fear of cheaper production with cheaper labor in other countries?*

JKG: On balance, I would judge multinationalism to be a force against tariffs. You don't need them if you own the foreign competitor. But also for the big firm producing in many countries tariffs are a nuisance. I've always thought the EEC – the Common Market – came into existence not because of a sudden burst of free-trade enlightenment but because the big multinational corporations had reached the point where internal trade barriers within Europe were a real handicap in doing business.

As a matter of fact, the multinational corporation not only works against tariffs but also, quite possibly, against more serious forms of international conflict.

NICOLE: *How?*

JKG: In the last century international tension was of real advantage to the great and mainly national corporations, those, for example, in mining and heavy industry in France and Germany. Tension produced orders for guns, steel and coal and was altogether good for business. So there was at least a temptation to stir up trouble or welcome it when it came along. Once a corporation begins operating in a highly visible way across international frontiers, it can no longer play that game. Or even be suspected of doing so.

NICOLE: *I always get back to the same thing. Does the multinational corporation have an effect on inflation and unemployment? Is it a cause?*

JKG: I don't think that the corporation, by being multinational, adds anything to the danger of inflation – beyond what occurs as the result of the passage of power to the technostructure. On whether it causes unemployment or not, there will be more debate. From time immemorial imports have been held to displace domestic products and the men who made them. If we import textiles into the United States from Japan, Taiwan, Hong Kong, jobs are lost to American workers. Textile employers who have never been known to feel the slightest compassion for any worker on any previous occasion now dissolve in sorrow over the loss of jobs. A truly pitiful grief. And if multinational corporations manufacture television sets in Japan and Taiwan, as they do, this similarly is said to take jobs away from American workers. But the consequence of both transactions is that we sell more of other products to those countries and thus have more employment in the industries that produce them. It would be hard to show any net loss of jobs from the tendency of the multinational corporation to seek the cheapest places of production.

NICOLE: *So we must look elsewhere for the causes of unemployment?*

JKG: Absolutely. We must look at the way we now control inflation by creating unemployment.

NICOLE: *But first there is money.*

JKG: Yes, that should come next.

NICOLE: *Can I understand money?*

JKG: Easily. It's merely the part of our subject matter on which, as economists, we make the greatest use of mystic rites and priestly incantation. I will gladly lead you into the temple.

Chapter 6

What About Money and Monetary Policy?

NICOLE: *So many questions are asked about money. Why should I try to understand it?*

JKG: As always, the essentials aren't very difficult. And it's important to understand it. We saw, when we talked earlier, that the power of the technostructure depends on its monopoly of knowledge. Banks and the financial community will have a similar monopoly if you leave all knowledge of money to them. And you can by no means be sure that this monopoly will work to your advantage. It might, as we've seen earlier, work to the advantage of the bankers. It's especially important that no one be put off by the fraudulent air of mystery that surrounds all questions having to do with banks and money.

NICOLE: *It's been said that the history of money is just the history of inflation. Is this true?*

JKG: Money has a long history. So has inflation. But the association is not complete. For most of the last century, for example, the trend of prices was down.

NICOLE: *Where does the history begin?*

JKG: No one really knows; the use of money antedates written history. Herodotus attributes the invention of coined money to the Greeks – the Lydians – along with some innovative forms of prostitution. But that's because he had no way of knowing of its far earlier use in India and perhaps elsewhere.

The history of money divides into three stages. In the first, what we may call original or basic money is in use. This is gold, silver or some other intrinsically desirable commodity. In the second stage, governments and banks become a major factor in the money supply – sometimes, in the case of the banks, without quite realizing it. But a basic commodity can still be had in specified quantity in exchange for government paper, bank notes or deposits. Thus the reference to a gold or silver standard. In the third and final stage, the metallic standard disappears; money becomes strictly a creation of the banks and the central banks and in consequence of what the government borrows. I don't think you can fully understand money without looking at this history and the way the use of money and its management have developed over time. Your mind assembles the details as, in fact, they were added over the centuries. When you get down to our own day, you have acquired the whole story more or less as it actually unfolded; you have been able to absorb and master each new complexity as it came along. Maybe it would be a good idea to take a few minutes to go a little further into this history.

NICOLE: *So how did things work in the first stage?*

JKG: The first stage is marvelously simple – as things should be. It was a bit awkward for somebody who had a sheep and wanted the latest in a loincloth to find a man who had a nice line of loincloths and wanted a sheep. So from well before the beginning of history, people settled on some convenient intermediate commodity that was portable, durable and divisible, which they could take for whatever they had to sell. This they could then hold and carry to the person from whom they wanted to buy something. Or they could simply hold on to it as a way of possessing something valuable. All this gives rise to the more tedious clichés of the textbooks. Money is an intermediate in the exchange process and thus a 'medium of exchange'. It measures the value of other things in exchange, is a 'standard of value'. Since it can be held, it is also a 'store-house of value'. Millions of students have been afflicted with these phrases, and they are quite true.

It's also quite true, as a very few economists have said – Thorstein Veblen and most recently my friend Wallace Peterson of the University of Nebraska – that an enormous number of people want money for its own sake, for the satisfaction and self-gratification and self-assurance its successful pursuit and possession give them.

But to get back to the history. The most convenient, portable and divisible of the intermediate commodities were, of course, the metals – silver, gold and copper in that order of importance. Silver, through most of history, was more important than gold. It's been thought, as I've said on other occasions, that because Judas sold Jesus for thirty pieces of silver, there was something derogatory about the transaction. There wasn't; silver was then the normal means of payment and so it was a very regular piece of business.

NICOLE: *Could one have inflation in the first stage?*

JKG: Within limits, yes. Prices depended, essentially, on the amount of business to be done on the one hand and on the abundance or the scarcity of the basic money, the gold or silver, on the other. That's another elementary proposition – in primitive form, the quantity theory of money. The more metal there was, given the volume of transactions and the rate at which people spent their money, the less it would buy and the higher would be the prices. After the discovery of the Americas, the mines of Mexico and Peru poured a large quantity of precious metals, mostly silver, into Europe. It came from Indian labor in the mines, not from the accumulated treasure of the Aztecs and the Incas. In consequence, prices were very high, which is to say there was inflation. For a couple of hundred years after the founding of the American colonies, tobacco was the basic money in Virginia and Maryland. At certain times there was a serious overproduction, and, in consequence, it took a lot of tobacco to buy clothing, food, whiskey and other essentials of life or to get a ship passage back to England. This, too, was inflation. But there were limits, generous as to the amount of tobacco that could be grown, more confining as to the amount of silver that could be mined. So with basic money – the first stage – inflation was limited as to extent and as to time.

NICOLE: *How do government and the banks come into the picture – your second stage?*

JKG: Governments took over the coinage of metal fairly early. And in China, beginning in the dimly distant past, governments began issuing paper notes in lieu of coins. Then it was discovered – first in Massachusetts in the Occident – that more notes could be issued than there was metal to redeem them. That was because people would carry the notes around and not try to turn them in so long as they were fairly certain they could get the hard money if they tried. The extra notes so issued increased the money supply, and, more to the point, they paid the government's bills just as well as did silver or gold. You can see how much more attractive this means of payment was than levying taxes.

NICOLE: *And the banks?*

JKG: They also became a way of increasing the money supply, and outside the Orient they began doing so long before governments did. Eventually they became a much more important source. The Romans had a well-developed banking system – but let me begin with a period on which we have better information. In the Italian Renaissance cities and later in Amsterdam and the other trading towns of northern Europe, people wanted a place where their money could be weighed – coins were clipped and otherwise debased – and kept in reasonable safety, a place of deposit. Thus the banks. Frequently the first private bankers were the goldsmiths because they had the best strongboxes.

Very soon the banks discovered that they could lend these

deposits to somebody else and charge interest. The borrower got a deposit which he could use as money or, the more frequent case, he was given bank notes certifying that he had the proceeds of the loan on deposit at the bank. The notes he could then pass on for whatever he needed to buy. The original depositor still had his deposit, his money. The man who borrowed also had money. You see that the bank, by making the loan, had created money. So it was then, and so it has been ever since. Money is created by a bank, now usually in the form of checking deposits, as a normal consequence of lending. When Mr Bert Lance gave himself those famous overdrafts, he created money, which, of course, he then spent. Creating money was about the only thing he wasn't accused of doing; maybe he was fortunate that no one thought of it. But, appropriately, it was the Comptroller of the Currency who ran him down.

NICOLE: *What about the gold standard?*

JKG: Or the silver standard – the principle is the same in either case. Let us stick with gold. The gold standard meant only that gold in specified weight would be given on demand for notes or deposits, including the extra ones resulting from the loans or the extra government paper I mentioned earlier. As long as both the original depositor and the man who had borrowed didn't come at the same time, the bank could do this. So could the public treasurer if his notes reflected only a considered excess over the gold on hand. As long as the metal was being paid to the people who came for it, the country was on the gold standard. Were there a run on the banks and if it continued long enough – too many people coming at the same time – there obviously wouldn't be enough gold to pay off everyone. And the same thing happened if too many people hit the government for the hard cash. Payment in gold would then have to be suspended. A war or some similar emergency might also force loans and money creation by the government in excess of what the gold reserves could ever be expected to cover.

So again the promise of gold payment would have to be suspended. In both cases the country would be said to have gone off the gold standard. That, I might add, was a fairly traumatic thing. When people read that their country had gone off gold, they looked at the heavens and expected them to fall.

NICOLE: *How long did it last, the gold standard?*

JKG: It achieved a very great reputation in the course of a relatively short life. Like Mozart or maybe not so much like Mozart. Gold was always well regarded, and in some periods and places it was the basic money, not silver. The Byzantines, who dominated trade between East and West for centuries, preferred gold, as their ornamentation still suggests. But it was not until 1867 that the European states got together in Paris and agreed that gold would henceforth be the reserve against deposits and note circulation and the means of payment between countries. The United States then abandoned silver six years later, an action that precipitated the great silver controversy and gave William Jennings Bryan his major issue in at least two of his three tries for the presidency. So the modern gold standard dates from the sixties and seventies of the last century. It was suspended in Europe during the First World War because of large purchases in the United States paid for in gold, partly rehabilitated after the war and abandoned for good in the Great Depression. At most, it had a sixty- or seventy-year run.

NICOLE: *Then why do people still attach such a great importance to gold?*

JKG: Well, John Maynard Keynes thought it was Freudian, that there was a deep affinity between men and gold that had overtones of sex. This has always seemed to me a trifle imaginative. I have an established ethnic respect for money, and I have always been appreciative of lovely women. There has anciently been a relationship between the two, but I have difficulty in thinking of them in precisely the same terms.

Mostly gold is important because it is so deeply a part of our history, though pecuniary interest is also involved. People who own or mine gold are likely to speak well of it. Swiss bankers do. South Africans certainly hope that it will retain its value and even be restored as money. Also, a liking for gold is in keeping with the natural conservatism of many people. If something was so revered in the past, it must still be good.

NICOLE: *If gold is obsolete as money, is it still a good investment?*

JKG: One should never advise other people on their investments – not without compensation. If the investment turns out well, they think it's their own wisdom; if it goes sour, they remember who gave them the bad advice. From 1933 until a couple of years ago, Americans were protected from either gain or loss; they were forbidden by law to hold gold. The law was passed early in the presidency of Franklin Roosevelt.

NICOLE: *Why?*

JKG: The gold content of the dollar was being lowered in the hope that this would raise prices. In other words, the amount of gold available for a paper dollar was being reduced and the number of dollars that could be issued against an ounce of gold was being increased. The action would have given a profit in dollars to people who held gold – more precisely, to a relatively small number of banks, individuals and speculators who had turned in their paper and deposits for gold. Roosevelt, by forbidding the private possession of gold, required them to turn in their holdings at the old exchange value in dollars. The law was repealed in 1975 at the behest of then-Senator James Buckley of New York, the brother of William Buckley, the famous conservative and humorist. On the day of repeal, Senator Buckley was first in line at the bank to buy some gold. For a long while he must have been sad; the price went down and down. However, if inflation continues, he will get his money back.

NICOLE: *Why was the gold standard abandoned during the Depression?*

JKG: It was according to the book; too many people came at the same time to the banks for the gold.

NICOLE: *What is the third stage in the history of money?*

JKG: The third comes after the gold standard. Banks are now permanently relieved of the obligation to pay gold to their depositors. And, needless to say, government paper can no longer be turned in for a specified amount of the metal. The regulation of the supply of money becomes exclusively a function of the central banks, of the Federal Reserve System, the Bank of England and the Bank of France. And this regulation, precisely as you would expect, is through control of the borrowing from the ordinary or commercial banks, for that, overwhelmingly, is now the way money gets created.

NICOLE: *How do the central banks control lending by the ordinary banks?*

JKG: Variously. American practice, which I use best for illustration, requires the commercial banks to maintain a specified reserve of cash – that being now the irredeemable government currency – against their deposits. If the banks seem to be lending too freely, creating too much money in the resulting new deposits, the Federal Reserve – the central bank – can raise the reserve requirement. That, obviously, puts a crimp in what the banks can safely lend. Or, more commonly, the Federal Reserve sells from its inventory of government securities, an inventory which is always fairly large. When people and institutions buy these securities, they take cash – reserves, in other words – from the commercial banks to pay the Federal Reserve. That also reduces what the banks can lend. These are what is called open-market operations – often thought a great mystery but, in fact, as you see, very simple. If their reserves are now too low, the banks can replenish them by borrowing from the Federal Reserve. But this can be discouraged by raising the interest rate. And since the banks will pass this higher rate on to their customers, that is presumed to discourage their borrowing, too. When you control the borrowing in this fashion, you control the creation of deposits and so you control the money supply – or at least what is by far the largest item in the money supply.

If there seems to be a need to increase the money supply, what would *you* do?

NICOLE: *Wouldn't you put the whole machinery into reverse? Reduce those reserve requirements; have the central bank buy securities instead of sell; lower interest rates, encourage borrowing and so have an increase in deposits. That would mean more money.*

JKG: Absolutely correct. You are now qualified as a central banker.

NICOLE: *I can hardly believe it. What has happened to all the gold in the meantime?*

JKG: Well, some of it is still stored in Fort Knox in the United States. Some is held by the International Monetary Fund – and sometime in these conversations you must ask me about that institution. Some is in jewelry, some in people's teeth. Some is still in the central banks. The Swiss have a goodly supply, as you might expect. Some gold also belongs to those people who think it's a good investment, will rise in price. Some is held against the day when everything else is expected to go phut but there will still be that lovely yellow metal. When that day comes, and I would urge all precautions against it, there may be some disappointment. Food will be the thing and warm clothing. Gold will be hard to eat and cold to wear.

NICOLE: *What counts as money now? Paper money, to be sure. But aren't there different kinds of bank deposits? What about savings deposits?*

JKG: This is a matter of highly learned debate. Everyone agrees that bank notes, Federal Reserve notes, notes of the Bank of England or franc notes are money. Everybody also agrees that bank deposits against which you can issue checks are money. On savings accounts there is some debate, although they probably qualify. Some argue that a person with a credit card has an implicit bank deposit with, say, American Express or Diners Club that is as good as money and is therefore money. Let us not pursue this too far; you can understand money and its creation without knowing exactly what should be included. The debate over what should be counted as money is between people who do not know and people who do not know that they do not know. Similarly, if you read that the money supply has increased or decreased during the past week or month, you should pay no attention whatsoever. Such short-run movements have no meaning. The experts debate their significance precisely because no one knows their significance.

NICOLE: *You say that the central banks manage money by open-market operations, by increase or decrease of reserves, by raising or lowering interest rates. Isn't that an arbitrary power? Who controls the central bank?*

JKG: It *is* an arbitrary power and one that has been a particular subject for discussion over the years. One school of thought has always held that so great is the power, it should be kept free from political influence, which is to say that it should be subject primarily to the influence of bankers and other insiders. They are presumed to be righteously above self-interest. This thought is reinforced by tradition. In the last century the Bank of England had substantial independence from the British government, and almost everything we now know about central banking was originally learned by the Bank of England. The Bank of France once had the same kind of independence. Accordingly, when the Federal Reserve System was established in the United States just before the outbreak of the First World War, it was given similar autonomy, and the thought that the President, as well as the Congress, should never interfere still persists. Control should be by bankers or experts or possibly by God but never by the government of the day.

NICOLE: *You do not agree?*

JKG: The independence is largely a myth. Such of it as exists is without justification. The Chairman of the Federal Reserve does not often turn down a direct request of the President. In meetings in the early sixties, one or two of which I remember well, the then-Chairman of the Federal Reserve (it was William McChesney Martin, but his name, like that of most central bankers, is now largely lost to history) would carefully remind the President and the others present of his special and independent responsibility. Then, when really pressed, he would say, 'Well, Mr President, I'll see what can be done.' The Bank of England and the Bank of France are fairly directly under the control of the government, and that is as it should be. Someone must be held responsible for economic policy. The worst possible position is when the President can blame the Federal Reserve for what goes wrong – inflation or unemployment. And the Federal Reserve Chairman can blame the President or protest that he is only doing his duty. In the United States it is the President who must be held responsible. And in other countries responsibility must be with the highest elected official. Money and banking are not superior to democracy.

NICOLE: *Until around twenty-five years ago, I've read, there wasn't much talk about money policy. Why was that?*

JKG: Before the Great Depression most economists felt that monetary policy could be a decisive force in regulating both prices and employment, prices in particular. If prices were falling and unemployment was rising, the central bank would lower interest rates, buy government securities and thus provide the commercial banks with lots of reserves from which to make loans. Money would thus be created and spent; demand in the economy as a whole would be expanded. Investment and output would be increased, prices would be strengthened, the unemployed would be brought into jobs. But in the Depression years it didn't work. Business was so bad that people didn't want to borrow money, however easy the terms. Why borrow to produce and sell at a loss? So in all countries there was a great diminution of faith in monetary policy, in what could be accomplished by managing the money supply through the central bank. And after the Depression came the Second World War. Then if loans were needed either by the government or by private firms for war production, as of course they were, they had to be provided. No one could then imagine that the central banks were a law unto themselves. Central-bank policy was made wholly subordinate to the needs of the war.

There was, therefore, a period from roughly 1930 until well after the Second World War when the central banks were largely irrelevant. What mattered was what governments borrowed and spent for unemployment, for then borrowing didn't depend on making a profit. Or later the decisive question was what had to be borrowed and spent for the purposes of the war. Monetary policy was secondary to public spending and tax policies, to what we call fiscal policy.

NICOLE: *I understand why it didn't work during the Depression, but can't it prevent inflation? And is this why it came back into fashion?*

JKG: To some extent, yes. In the 1950s, rising prices, modest by recent standards, became a problem. Monetary policy – action which could be taken without legislation by quiet, calm gentlemen sitting around a large table in the Federal Reserve Building or the Bank of England or the Bank of France – seemed a wonderfully convenient way of solving it.

NICOLE: *And doesn't monetary policy deal with inflation?*

JKG: It does. If the central bank tightens up sufficiently on the commercial banks so that it affects decisively the money they have to lend and forces them to lend what they do lend at high interest rates, there will obviously be less spending, less demand in the economy. In particular, there will be less money to build houses, for other construction, for smaller business investment in inventories, plant and equipment and for installment purchases of automobiles and household appliances because all of these things are financed by bank borrowing. If this restraint on borrowing – on creation of deposits to be spent and respent – is pressed hard enough, it will stop inflation.

But now we must go back to our discussion of the other day. The effect of this restraint will always be highly unequal. It works, let me repeat, through restricting the aggregate of spending in the economy, restricting what economists call aggregate demand. When this restriction in demand hits General Motors, Exxon, Philips, Shell or the other large corporations, it doesn't force them to stop raising prices. They first cut back on sales and production. We've already seen that they have the power to resist price reductions. It's one of the reasons they want to be big. And if their wage costs are going up or there is other justification for raising prices, they will do so. They will only be forced to stop raising prices and forced to resist wage increases when there is a lot of idle capacity. By then there will be a good deal of unemployment. And this will also help restrain union demands. So, for these large firms, monetary policy works by creating unemployment. And that, of course, has been the highly visible consequence of its recent use.

It has another effect – what amounts to another favor for the strong and against the weak. The large corporation, we saw, has a source of capital independent of the banks. That is from its own earnings, and resort to this source is not affected by central-bank restrictions on lending by the commercial banks. In any case, the big firms are the favorite customers of the banks, the first to be served if there is any money to be lent. Since they control their prices, they can also pass higher interest rates on to their customers. So they are very well protected against the adverse effects of monetary policy. In contrast, the farmer, the small tradesman who needs money to carry his inventories and, above all, firms in industries like housing which operate on borrowed money and depend on customers who borrow money are highly vulnerable to monetary policy. So you see how it works – by creating unemployment, by exempting the big and strong corporations and by putting the squeeze on the small and the weak.

NICOLE: *Then why is monetary policy still recommended by economists?*

JKG: There has always been a certain fascination among economists with the mechanics of central-bank policy. It's our profession's special form of magic. This has led some to overlook its highly discriminatory effect. But, in general and quite rightly, it is the favored measure of very conservative people.

NICOLE: *Such as Milton Friedman?*

JKG: Yes. Professor Friedman is a very attractive and persuasive man, but he is an avowed conservative, and it is not the function of a conservative to worry about policies that favor big business over small business. Or about unemployment. He does not, and it is his privilege to ignore these adverse effects. However, I don't want to make Friedman sound altogether heartless, and this takes us back to an earlier point. More than most, Milton Friedman has a vision of an economy that is made up of competitive firms ruled by the market. For him the market still lives, and the great and powerful corporation has never been important in his thinking. If you grant him his view of economic life – competition in a still effective market – although it does take some understanding and tolerance, you see how monetary policy can be imagined to spread itself more or less uniformly over an economy of competitive firms. It can be supposed to treat all more or less alike, and, since the firms are competitive and subject to the impersonal forces of the market, a curtailment of bank lending and aggregate demand forces all to reduce prices or forgo price increases. This, not unemployment, is the first effect. And from this we get Friedman's central recommendation, which is that you limit lending and money creation so that the supply of money and the resulting demand increase only as the supply of goods and services increases or can be increased. Any tendency toward a greater increase in lending, money creation and demand is sternly controlled. The result is an economy of stable prices.

NICOLE: *Why isn't this so?*

JKG: We live in the real world. Monetary restriction doesn't stop the people who have escaped the discipline of the market and got control of their prices and incomes from shoving up those prices and incomes. They are stopped only when there is a lot of unemployment. Meanwhile it does work, in a rather punishing way, for those who are still subject to the market.

NICOLE: *Has Professor Friedman's remedy really been tried?*

JKG: Yes, though he would say imperfectly. If there were a perfect and possible design wholly to his specifications that worked and was reasonably painless, it would, of course, have been used before now. Every government would have seized upon it to the exclusion of all other policies. Politicians, however retarded, are not so stupid as to reject as convenient and simple a formula as Professor Friedman proposes. But there has been plenty of practical proof both of the unworkability and of the pain. Professor Friedman and his disciples were influential in the administrations of Presidents Nixon and Ford. Mr William Simon, Mr Ford's Secretary of the Treasury, and Mr Alan Greenspan, Chairman of Mr Ford's Council of Economic Advisers, along with Chairman Arthur Burns of the Federal Reserve, joined in making substantial use of monetary policy to slow (though not to stop) the great inflation of 1974–5. The result was a sharp cutback in production and a sharp increase in unemployment – a serious recession. There was particular distress in the housing industry; it had its worst slump since the Great Depression. Small business also had a hard time. All, in fact, was in accordance with the book. For Mr Simon and Mr Greenspan, as well as for Professor Friedman, the pain was not so great. For those who lost their jobs, it was not so agreeable, and that, of course, included Mr Ford. He was the first President since Herbert Hoover to be denied re-election. It was the economic policy that defeated him. Mr Ford is a decent and generous man; still, one wonders if he enjoyed being sacrificed for the economic faith of his advisers.

NICOLE: *Professor Friedman was, for a while, adviser to the government of Israel.*

JKG: Well, it is part of the ancient Hebraic lore that the children of Israel were meant to suffer.

NICOLE: *He also advised the Chilean government.*

JKG: He was much criticized because, just for a very few days, he went down to advise the government of Chile, the Chilean dictatorship. On this I defend him. There is no doubt, I think, about Professor Friedman's personal commitment to civil liberties. And, as one who would like to see the Chilean dictatorship come to an end, I can think of no better way than to have it follow Professor Friedman's advice. One must have a comprehensive view of these matters.

NICOLE: *I am still puzzled that so many people think monetary policy is useful and valid.*

JKG: Some, as I said before, are attracted by the convenience. It requires no legislation and can be used quickly without a lot of tedious debate. On occasion, governments have been forced back on monetary policy simply because, facing inflation, there seemed to be nothing else to do. So it has been at times in Britain. But, let me repeat, monetary policy is a natural and legitimate expression of conservatism. If you're not concerned about unemployment, if you don't like trade unions and if you favor large business over small businesses that depend on borrowed money – all legitimate political positions as long as so understood – you should be in favor of monetary policy.

NICOLE: *Doesn't monetary policy make the bankers happy? I would think they would like a higher rent on the money they lend.*

JKG: Oh, yes. This isn't often mentioned. Bankers, alone among businessmen, are supposed to raise their prices purely for reasons of economic statesmanship to prevent inflation. But they don't object at all to the higher return.

NICOLE: *I have another question about monetary policy. If it works by cutting back on borrowing for business investment, isn't that harmful? Doesn't it keep people from buying machinery and inventory, make business less productive?*

JKG: That I should have mentioned. Governments that have relied on monetary policy to prevent or limit inflation have done serious damage to business investment in their own countries. Again the British are a case in point. They have relied very heavily on monetary policy in the last fifteen or twenty years, and it is one reason why new plant investment in Britain has lagged, with an effect on labor productivity and costs. Economists have rather neglected the effect on productivity of restricting borrowing for investment by smaller firms.

NICOLE: *I want to go back to the Great Depression for a moment, when monetary policy was discarded. What then took its place?*

JKG: Fiscal policy – the budget. When governments couldn't get people to borrow from the banks, spend money and stimulate demand and the economy in this fashion, they began borrowing and spending themselves. That made it certain that the money got borrowed and got spent. And, in reverse, when they needed to control inflation, it was thought that higher taxes would keep people from spending their own money and reduced public expenditures would keep the government from adding to demand. So governments used the budget instead of monetary policy to regulate total or aggregate demand in the economy and thus prevent unemployment or inflation.

NICOLE: *Why didn't that work?*

JKG: Let's take that up next time.

Chapter 7

What is Fiscal Policy?

NICOLE: *Exactly what is fiscal policy?*

JKG: Before I answer, perhaps we should have a short reminder. We saw yesterday that monetary policy seeks to control the economy by regulating the amount of borrowing from the banks and the spending and respending of the money so created. It expands aggregate demand for goods and services, if that is indicated, by having more spending from borrowed money. If the need is to restrain spending because of the danger of inflation, then the central bank can cut back on spending from borrowed funds. And we saw why this doesn't work It didn't deal reliably with unemployment in the Great Depression. And, more to the point now, it is an exceptionally painful remedy for inflation for those least able to stand the pain. It is effective only as it produces unemployment; and to stop inflation there must be a lot of such unemployment.

The past alternative, although no policies are mutually exclusive, was to control aggregate demand through fiscal measures. These work through the management of the government budget. If there is unemployment, you cut taxes; that leaves people with more private income to spend and the resulting demand means more jobs. Or you increase public expenditures without increasing taxes, and so the government adds to demand with the same effect. Furthermore, the people the government employs spend and add more to demand – what economists call the multiplier effect. If inflation is the problem, you put the policy into reverse. You raise taxes, and this cuts down on private spending. You cut back on public expenditures, and that means the government contributes less to the demand for goods and services, reduces aggregate demand.

NICOLE: *Is fiscal policy now the accepted way to manage the economy?*

JKG: In the industrial countries it has been the mainstream policy in principle at least, since the Second World War. Political preference has some influence here. Conservatives, for good reason as we've seen, lean to monetary policy. Liberal economists in the United States and social democrats in Europe have generally leaned toward fiscal policy. But those who advocate fiscal policy don't exclude some use of monetary policy. And those who love monetary policy always urge budget restraint or a balanced budget. Otherwise government borrowing, by expanding the money supply in the same way as does private borrowing, nullifies their effort.

NICOLE: *I don't see how you can have fiscal policy and a balanced budget. But President Carter has repeatedly promised this balance. So did Giscard d'Estaing until very recently. Are they opposed to fiscal policy?*

JKG: You cannot have an active fiscal policy and a balanced budget. If there is idle capacity and unemployment, the government must spend more than it receives in taxes, have a budget deficit. And, conceivably, if inflation is serious and people and business firms are spending money out of their savings, then you might want to compensate with an over-balanced budget, a budget surplus. So there is no merit at all in a policy that just balances income and outgo, none whatever. That, by the way, is fortunate. In the United States we haven't had a balanced budget since 1969. The last before that was for 1960.

NICOLE: *Then why do politicians promise a balanced budget?*

JKG: They also come out for truth, marital fidelity, lower taxes, efficient government, peace and the sanctity of motherhood. It's a conventional virtue. Its affirmation places you on the side of the saints and in opposition to Satan but has no practical significance.

I gather that President Giscard has now dropped his promise of a balanced budget. President Carter hasn't done so, but I promise you that his economists don't take it all that seriously. They believe, perhaps excessively, in fiscal policy. So, whatever they may say or not say in public, they regard the balanced budget as a conventional obeisance, a harmless prudential overture to an ancient faith.

NICOLE: *But is it practical to say you're going to raise taxes and reduce public spending? Won't people resist?*

JKG: Fiercely. And here we come to the first difficulty with fiscal policy – the huge gap between what seems possible in theory and what *is* possible in practice. Most of the advocates of fiscal policy are, alas, living in the past. In the mass-consumption society, occupational restraints on consumption break down. Blue-collar workers, white-collar workers, minorities, press a claim to items of consumption once thought proper only for the affluent and the privileged. Television has had something to do with it. Also improving educational standards. The democratic ethic has probably been most important of all. There has always been a problem here. People are told that all are born equal. But then they must be told that to ask for equality in economic enjoyments is inconsistent with the natural operation of the free enterprise system and possibly subversive as well. In recent times they have become less and less persuaded of the logic of this argument. So, while there are still great class differences in consumption, there are not as many as there used to be. Almost everyone asserts a claim to an automobile, a liveable house, non-lethal health care. University education in my youth was confined, as a matter of course, to the sons of clergymen and the well-to-do; in most industrially advanced countries it is now a human right. Formerly only leisured Americans made a trip to Europe; now it is widely

east once in a lifetime you will have a holiday
land or Italy or make a visit to the old coun-
nat was. In consequence, it is very difficult to
order to reduce private spending; it runs against
social current and invites mass opposition.

It's almost equally difficult to reduce public expenditures.
The things that the state provides are also part of our standard
of living. This part of the living standard is slightly more vulnerable because public education, public housing, public
health care, various social expenditures, all help to bring the
consumption levels of the less affluent up toward those of the
more fortunate. Many people of means are naturally indignant
over the waste in such spending. They speak vehemently of the
failure of government officials to see their clear duty and to cut
public outlays, a few things like defense, air safety and necessary business services apart. They don't always see, though
some do, that public expenditures buy for the poor the education, recreation, health care, housing, even the protection
against crime, that the affluent are able to provide for themselves.

NICOLE: *Isn't this difference between theory and reality rather
obvious?*

JKG: It should be. But an older generation of economists and
a younger generation of reputable conformists, all still influential in the textbooks and classrooms, do not perceive the power
of the non-economic forces, the political and social forces, with
which they are contending. So they still talk easily about raising taxes or reducing public expenditures to regulate aggregate
demand. It's my impression, or anyhow hope, that a more innovative younger group sees the problem rather more clearly.

NICOLE: *Couldn't the government possibly reduce military expenditures? They're a big part of government spending.*

JKG: But that's the income of the weapons producers and the
military establishment, who would surely object. When there

is discussion of the reduction of public expenditures, it is almost always assumed that it is civilian expenditures that should be trimmed. And among civilian expenditures, it is those for welfare and to aid the people of the urban ghettos – George Bernard Shaw's undeserving poor – that are believed to reflect the greatest waste. Again the seemingly sound and righteous policy is what punishes the weakest and the poorest, who also, more than incidentally, are the least articulate. Military expenditures, needed or otherwise, are defended by strong corporations, formidable generals, a big bureaucracy. So they are never imagined to be subject to reduction for reasons of fiscal policy. An increase, conceivably, but never a decrease.

NICOLE: *Then assuming that taxes can't be raised and that state spending can't be reduced, can fiscal policy work?*

JKG: It works well only in one direction. You can reduce taxes if there's unemployment, and, with more difficulty, you can raise public expenditures if there is unemployment. In recent years one group of American fiscal-policy experts has made advocacy of tax reduction a kind of liturgy. It being the only thing that is possible and applauded, they ask for it on all occasions for all ills. Professor Walter Heller, one of the great pioneers in this field, Chairman of the Council of Economic Advisers under both Presidents Kennedy and Johnson and altogether a very distinguished man, eventually became so enchanted with tax reduction that, it was said, he came to prescribe it for chronic nose drip. He and others advised reducing taxes at the very peak of the inflation in the United States in 1974 and 1975. I urged raising them. That was logical but, in the event, equally ill-timed. Before Congress could get around to it, the tight-money policy I mentioned had brought on the recession.

NICOLE: *I see the difficulty. Raising taxes and reducing public expenditures aren't so easy in France either. But what would happen if you could do these things? Would it cure inflation?*

JKG: If pressed hard enough and against all the outcry, expenditure cuts and tax increases would reduce public and private spending and cut back on aggregate demand – demand for all goods and services. But fiscal policy also has a discriminatory effect; and it operates very differently in different parts of the economy. In the half dominated by the large corporations there is, as we have so often seen, the power to control prices – to resist price reduction and increase prices if costs go up. So the first effect of a reduction or curtailment of demand in this part of the economy is on sales, production and employment. As with monetary policy, price increases here are only arrested when there is a good deal of idle capacity and enough unemployment to make the unions forgo wage increases. Meanwhile fiscal policy does work against the small businessman and the farmer. So again the sad fact. Even if fiscal policy could be applied with rigor against inflation, it would work by creating the equal, opposite and maybe greater evil, which is unemployment. And it would work by lowering the prices of farmers and small firms that are still subject to the market and therefore do not have control over their prices.

In the present year (1977) inflation has fallen to a relatively low level in the United States, and my economist friends in Washington have indulged themselves in a fair amount of self-congratulation. I don't blame them for that. An economist in high office needs to congratulate himself these days, for, given the level of accomplishment, no one else will. But no congratulations have come from American farmers. That is because such reductions in the rate of inflation as have been achieved have come from the effect of restriction in aggregate demand on farm prices – and from good crops. The government's economic policy has had no visible effect on wages and industrial prices. There inflation has been reliable and persistent.

NICOLE: *Are you saying that instead of having inflation followed by recession – the old-fashioned business cycle – we have today inflation, recession and unemployment at the same time?*

JKG: That's right. With fiscal policy or monetary policy or both, we curb inflation by creating a recession and unemployment. And, as I've said, it takes a good deal of unemployment to prevent inflation. Whoever arranged matters this way is open to criticism.

Modern recessions, by the way, are interesting. Even when caused deliberately by monetary or fiscal policy, they are still thought to be a natural phenomenon, a manifestation of the classical cycle I just mentioned. Only the recovery, if and when it comes, is considered to be the work of human hands and economic intelligence. President Ford's economists, Messrs Simon, Greenspan and Burns, whom I mentioned earlier, slowed down the great inflation of 1974–5 by bringing on the worst recession since the Great Depression. This was attributed to the natural ebb of the business cycle. Later they and their successors praised themselves for engineering a commendably rapid recovery. A good business.

NICOLE: *Going back to fiscal policy: why do economists still rely on it? As you say, the textbooks still claim that it is the proper policy.*

JKG: Again the inevitable lag behind events. In the aftermath of the Great Depression and after the Second World War, fiscal policy as I have described it did seem to work, for about twenty years. Inflation then was not seriously a problem. One can argue as to the reasons. Corporations were still being cautious in wage settlements. They had not yet realized how easily these increases could be passed along; there was still some tendency to resist the unions as a manifestation of old-fashioned capitalist conviction. Unions, on their side, were less aggressive in their demands; there was still a residue of fear from the Depression years which made jobs, not pay, seem the important thing. In any case, these twenty years were the golden age of economics, and fiscal policy got the credit. In the last ten years, in virtually all of the industrial countries, inflation has been serious and persistent. Fiscal policy doesn't work or is too painful to use, but faith in the old magic lingers on.

NICOLE: *I still don't see why things got so much worse in the last ten years.*

JKG: I argued earlier that change in economic institutions is more rapid than we appreciate or like to believe. In addition to the changes I just mentioned, corporations continued to get larger and stronger. Unions became important in the United States in new fields, especially in the public services. Governments, as an aspect of responsive democracy in which we all rejoice, came to the support of new groups – the old, the minorities, the dependent, the ill. These were given, if not control of, at least protection for their income. All of this contributed further to the retreat from the market. And the market, let me repeat once again, is essential for effective fiscal as for effective monetary policy. Once people or organizations are in control of their own prices and incomes, there is no way that monetary or fiscal policy can keep them from increasing those prices and incomes except by creating unemployment and inducing a recession.

NICOLE: *What have American economists come up with?*

JKG: Mr Carter came to the presidency with a promise to reduce inflation sharply and to reduce unemployment. He brought into office the pick of the Establishment economists; on grounds of reputation no one could fault his choice. But, alas, until now, they have done almost nothing and nothing new. After nearly a year, unemployment is still high and inflation is increasing. It's an indication of how time has left the exponents of the traditional monetary or fiscal policy behind. To be an economic adviser is still a prestigious thing; even to be a failed adviser is rather good. We still hear constantly in the United States from Mr Nixon's and Mr Ford's economists on what we should do. I am naturally proud of being an economist, and for that reason I would like to see our profession held to far higher standards of performance.

In fact, there are a fair number of non-official economists who are discussing new lines of policy. But, as we talk, those in official position are still hoping that the old policies will work. Or they are resorting secretly to prestidigitation, incantation, table-turning and other dubious practices to reconcile low unemployment with less inflation.

NICOLE: *You have advocated control of prices and wages.*

JKG: Yes, in a dreary, repetitive way, but only because of the worse alternatives. I've also come to believe that more fundamental action is necessary as well. Most economists now do agree that wages shove up prices, that the large corporations can pass the higher costs on to the public, and that the resulting wage/price spiral *is* a central cause of present-day inflation. The gap, once again, is between understanding and action, between reality and hope. To control prices arouses the opposition of the people whose prices are controlled. To limit wage increases encounters the opposition of the unions. And this opposition should surprise no one. The unions' resistance lies in the universal desire to control one's income. Who wants to escape from control by the market to control by the state? Wage control, like taxation or reduced public expenditure, acts against the great social thrust for higher consumption. You can understand how economists would wish to avoid the row that this policy would precipitate. Even more the politicians for whom they work.

NICOLE: *Why have you advocated it?*

JKG: I am not in public office, and it's not necessary for me to cultivate the applause of corporations and trade unions. And I've always had a mild pleasure in controversy – a perverse and slightly depraved personality, I'm led to believe. But I also think that direct control must be part of a larger policy in which restraint is both general and equitable. Could we come to that tomorrow?

NICOLE: *Certainly. But I want to go back to unemployment for a moment. I've heard it said that the skills and training of the labor force have a great deal to do with unemployment. What about that?*

JKG: Yes, what we call the structure of the labor force is very important. We have been talking about unemployment as though all workers were interchangeable, and, of course, they're not. There are workers with different skills and different levels of experience, and a very large number with no skills and no work experience at all. And there are locations where workers are wanted and others – the ghettos inhabited by the minorities in the American cities – where there are no employers and no jobs available. In some job categories and some locations experienced workers can be very scarce and unions can readily get increases. Wages will even be bid up by employers who need particular skills. And in other areas unskilled young workers who have no experience in the labor market will still be unemployed in huge numbers. In the United States many of these are black, Spanish-speaking or female. So there now can be full employment, even great scarcity, in parts of the labor market and severe unemployment in other parts.

NICOLE: *What can be done about it?*

JKG: All education increases mobility. So does the elimination of discrimination against minorities. So do training and re-training; there is no case for planning so strong as that for anticipating needed skills and encouraging and financing appropriate preparation.

NICOLE: *Why are unemployment and inflation so different in different countries if the causes are the same? Germany and Switzerland have much lower rates than those in the United States and Britain.*

JKG: Unemployment has, in fact, increased somewhat in Germany in recent times. But circumstances do differ. Germany in the 1920s had a very grim experience with inflation; the result was a deep scar on the German psyche. Americans remember the Great Depression; Germans remember the Great Inflation. In consequence, German trade unions, when they bargain, are much more open than American or British unions to arguments on the danger of inflation. So Germany and also Austria have a built-in restriction on wage claims, an implicit, self-administered system of wage restraint. So does Switzerland, perhaps more out of natural discipline and conservatism.

There is another factor, highly important and not much discussed. Germany and Switzerland park their unemployed labor outside their own borders; they then let workers in more or less as needed. Nearly a quarter of the Swiss labor force is from southern Italy, Spain and other countries. Almost 10 percent of the German labor force comes from Yugoslavia, Turkey, Italy. By allowing in roughly the number for whom there are jobs and refusing entry to workers when there is a surplus, it is possible to keep German and especially Swiss unemployment at a very low level. The people who do not get in are counted as unemployed in Yugoslavia, Italy, Turkey and Spain or maybe not counted anywhere. In Britain and the United States the unemployed are within the country and have to be counted there. Comparisons of those two countries with Germany and Switzerland are not valid.

NICOLE: *In France we consider a 5 percent rate of unemployment very high. How can you in the United States accept a level of 7 percent, which I read it was not very long ago?*

JKG: I have the impression that the French labor force has a smaller proportion of workers, corresponding to our young blacks and Puerto Ricans, without work experience or skills. But, like Switzerland and Germany, France, in a less organized way, relies on foreign workers – people from Portugal and North Africa. These come or do not come as jobs are available.

So part of the French unemployment is in Algeria, Tunisia, Morocco and Portugal. I say less organized. France is less adept than Switzerland or Germany in adjusting inflow to need, less successful in excluding or returning those it can't use.

NICOLE: *What about the socialist countries? Are there inflation and unemployment in the Soviet Union and Eastern Europe or in China?*

JKG: From brief observation, I would judge that the Chinese maintain a very close control both on their wages and on their total demand. Recently, you may have seen, they unfroze wages and allowed the first increase in fourteen years. That kind of control over the work force could turn a lot of old-fashioned capitalists to Communism. And unemployment is always less evident in an agricultural country; people divide up what work there is and work less hard. Disguised unemployment replaces the open statistical unemployment of the industrial economy and the factory system. The USSR and the socialist countries of Eastern Europe don't have much open unemployment, but they do have persistent inflation. People press, as in the West, for higher wages, higher salaries and more public services. So costs press on prices as they do with us. And there is a continuing excess of demand in relation to the supply of goods and services that are available. But in these countries inflation shows itself in a different form. Prices are generally fixed. Accordingly, inflation manifests itself not in higher prices but in longer queues, longer lines waiting for scarce goods. You beat inflation by getting there first and standing longer than your neighbor. It's not a wholly desirable solution in a cold climate.

NICOLE: *Why can't we learn to live with inflation, I mean in France or the United States?*

JKG: If we ever stopped trying to prevent inflation, we would surely have a lot of it. And this would be to accept grave injustice. One cause of inflation, we've seen, is that many people now have control or a measure of control over their incomes. Those with the best control can protect themselves by raising their prices and perhaps even improve their position. Those who have no control suffer and fall behind. Income distribution becomes increasingly lopsided in favor of the strong. The American figures are fairly good on this. With inflation, income is reallocated from the old to the people of middle years and from the poor to the rich. And, almost certainly, from workers who are not organized in unions to those who are. This isn't very compassionate or even very safe. I doubt that we'll ever have a violent revolt of the aged, but we know that we can have angry behavior in city ghettos by the poor, the black and the young.

Inflation also causes problems in accounting. You are no longer sure what your earnings are worth And, in making contracts, you don't know what your costs will be. There are also serious international complications; when different countries have different rates of inflation, exchange rates will be unstable. Let's talk about that later on.

So I have never thought we should accept inflation. Economists, I repeat, should be held to high standards of performance. They should be made to deal with both unemployment and inflation and be paid accordingly. They should not be allowed to escape into failure.

NICOLE: *Could inflation, under certain circumstances, still run away?*

JKG: Yes. But no one really knows how great the danger is. In the affluent countries people, at any time, have a large amount of spendable assets in their possession – bank deposits, savings deposits, cashable government bonds, currency tucked away under the floor or in the mattress. Should sharply rising prices ever persuade them that these assets were going to be worthless in the future, there could be a rush to spend. The result would be runaway inflation. A lesser inflation could cause a total one. Because we don't know how great the danger is, we shouldn't take risks.

NICOLE: *Was this what happened in Germany in the 1920s, a rush to spend?*

JKG: Essentially. In the later stages of the 1922–3 inflation, people lost all confidence in the purchasing power of the Reichsmark. They rushed to get rid of their money and other spendable assets, sometimes within minutes of receiving them. This was a cause of the inflation and a result of the inflation.

NICOLE: *What about indexing – having everybody's price or income go up with inflation?*

JKG: I have never been very happy about indexing. It involves technical problems. Also some inequities. And it is a surrender to inflation. Again I would make economists earn their living – produce proper remedies and not evade the problems.

NICOLE: *Could you enlarge? Why is indexing difficult and inequitable?*

JKG: Many kinds of income, pensions in particular, were fixed in the past by contract. There is now no one to pay the indexed increase or anyone who could properly be forced to do so. Many forms of savings could not be indexed, or not without great difficulty. And while indexing would help some people keep up with price increases, it would not prevent those who have greater power over their incomes from trying to get ahead of price increases. So, with indexing, you would have more inflationary pressure from people whose incomes would now go up with the index and just as much as now from people who want to gain on the price increases. The prospect, on balance, would be for more inflation than before. I say on balance, for you can't be absolutely sure; these things are difficult to predict, and you should remember that we economists compensate for great uncertainty of knowledge with great certainty of statement.

NICOLE: *Are you saying that both inflation and the usual remedies hurt the weak?*

JKG: Yes, that is the absolutely vital conclusion. Inflation hurts the weak and so do the orthodox measures for controlling it. Inflation takes from the old, the unorganized and the poor and gives to those who are strongly in control of their own incomes. Monetary policy works by putting people out of jobs and by depressing the prices of those who have the least control. Also, it denies loans to the smaller man, who depends on borrowed money for his business, but it gives the corporations which have capital from their own earnings a free run. Fiscal policy is somewhat more equitable than monetary policy. But it also works by restricting production and employment, and it does this before prices are affected. So it, too, puts the burden of controlling inflation on those who lose their jobs. It works better on the prices of small businessmen and farmers, those who are least able to maintain their prices and incomes.

NICOLE: *So monetary policy is easy and unjust, fiscal policy is difficult and unjust, controls are unpopular, and we can't have inflation or unemployment. Well, what do we do? Is the system bankrupt?*

JKG: A good, grim question. But don't be wholly pessimistic. The system lends itself, remember, to a lot of repair work.

Chapter 8

What's to Be Done?

NICOLE: *You've described a kind of circle. Unemployment is the remedy for inflation. To reduce unemployment is to get more inflation. Is there a solution? What you called a patch-up?*

JKG: Yes, and at first glance it looks like a very difficult one. But then we find it is the path that most countries are traveling in a tentative way. We find ourselves in the mainstream.

It will always be necessary to keep the total demand in the economy in some fairly close relationship to the supply of goods and services that can be made available when people are fully employed. And fiscal and monetary policy have a role in this, though it is more passive than active. As the economy expands, so will public and private spending from borrowed funds. This must be controlled so that total spending does not increase more rapidly than the readily available supply of goods. You control the increase in public spending from borrowed funds by fiscal policy, the increase in private spending by monetary policy.

None of this is too difficult. It requires principally a restraining hand on *increases* in bank lending and on public spending, although, on occasion, there might have to be more taxes on the affluent. This will always produce screams of outrage, but it is not politically impossible. In a growing economy one can maintain a balance between total demand in the economy and total supply without draconian measures of monetary and fiscal restraint.

This rough equivalence between total demand and total supply is the framework. But it is only the framework, since all who have escaped from the discipline of the market can still shove up their incomes and prices. To stop this without adding to unemployment is the remainder of the task, one that goes well outside the conventional limits of economics.

NICOLE: *You mean economic policy becomes political policy?*

JKG: At a minimum, economic policy becomes far more dependent on political skill than on economic wisdom.

NICOLE: *Could you explain more fully?*

JKG: As organizations, groups and individuals gain authority over their incomes, free themselves from the control of the market, they contribute to inflation in two ways. They raise their prices or wages, the most important dimension of income. Prices, including wages, for some are costs for others. So these increases directly shove up prices – what most economists have come to accept as cost-push inflation.

The second inflationary effect works through bank lending, a process not fully appreciated even by all economists. As costs push up prices, firms that operate on borrowed money need to borrow more. This is necessary if they are to do the same volume of business at the higher prices. So cost-push inflation and the general pressure on markets from higher incomes force the bank loans and the resulting increase in money supply that finance and allow the inflation. And to resist this demand for borrowed funds requires more than the passive restraint I mentioned earlier. It requires an active and painful monetary policy, one that punishes, as always, the weakest borrowers. So cost-push inflation causes an increase in bank lending and can't be cured except with great pain and very uneven effect by cutting back on such lending.

NICOLE: *Let me interrupt. You are saying that when wages shove up prices, the central bank must go along and allow more lending instead of forcing the contraction and unemployment that would prevent inflation.*

JKG: Yes. Although I use wages only as an example. Any successful upward pressure by a group on its income has the same effect.

NICOLE: *Then what do we do?*

JKG: The solution that is emerging has no generally accepted name. It recognizes that an uncontrolled struggle for more income brings an inflation that defeats some or most of these efforts and that the traditional methods of control – monetary and fiscal policy – either do not work or work by hurting the least affluent, the least employable, those with least control over their prices and incomes. This we've seen. And the solution accepts that no single group can carry the burden of restraint. It must be fairly distributed among all groups.

NICOLE: *I understand that. But how do you proceed as a practical matter?*

JKG: In practice governments begin with consultation. They seek agreement from the principal groups in the economy that they will hold their demands to affordable increases in income – increases that, on the whole, are consistent with stable prices and general social equity. This means that wage increases must be kept to what can be afforded without forcing up prices. It means also a companion price policy for the large corporations, one that does not take advantage of the pay restraint while allowing unavoidable cost increases to be passed along. This is another way of saying that profits must be kept in line with general past experience. And there must be a similar understanding and restraint on minimum wages, the pay of civil servants, farm support prices, pensions, transportation costs, other publicly-controlled incomes and prices. Understanding on these matters must be sought through government-led negotiation and conciliation. However, having done everything possible to reach a consensus, the government must also retain the power to enforce the result.

NICOLE: *You say this type of action has no name?*

JKG: Various terms have been used in the past to describe efforts along these lines – a new social contract, what in France has been called a new moral contract, incomes policy, wage and price policy, controls. Some of the terms have overtones of ineffectuality because their authors don't really wish to face the hard issues. I've used the word 'control' in the past so that no one would think there was an easy escape from firm government responsibility. I now propose that we try a new designation, one that is fairly descriptive, and speak of a Comprehensive Incomes and Prices Policy, a CIPP.

NICOLE: *This goes beyond what we ordinarily think of as control of wages and prices?*

JKG: Yes, much. It extends in principle to all who have achieved a measure of control over their incomes; after all, the escape from the control of the market is what makes it necessary in the first place. And it involves a variety of restraints. Trade union claims are limited to what can be afforded, on the average, from increased productivity. Then there is no general increase in labor costs. Large business corporations which now control their own prices – have opted out from control by the market – respect this wage restraint and do not increase *their* prices. Profits can still go up but only as these result from more sales or above-average gains in productivity or efficiency. This is not a very revolutionary step. It means only that public price restraints replace the private price-fixing of the large corporations.

The pay of civil servants, who are now a very important group, must be consistent with the general restraint. Here the government already has a strong hand or should have. Minimum farm prices, minimum wages and transportation costs are already set by public action. Farm prices are especially important because of their direct bearing on living costs. For basic crops the proper policy, now also generally accepted, is to maintain balancing reserves. These are accumulated when prices are low, thus sustaining prices, and sold when supplies are short, thus stabilizing prices. This principle underlies the new international wheat agreement which is now being negotiated.

Some price fluctuation for farm products is, of course, inevitable. And small industries, service enterprises, the self-employed, should not be controlled. Here the market, even though imperfect, still works.

NICOLE: *You are really taking a wage-limitation policy and widening it to include other groups.*

JKG: That's right. In the past a reference to an incomes policy meant a policy on union wages, mostly blue-collar wages. That was too easy and remarkably unfair. You can't limit the return of the man on the shop floor and leave that of the executive upstairs untouched. I should stress this point: a movement to greater fairness in income distribution is indispensably a part of a Comprehensive Incomes and Prices Policy.

NICOLE: *In France and some other countries it is being proposed that there be a specified differential between the lowest-paid worker and the highest-paid executive. Is that the way to handle executive salaries?*

JKG: Sooner or later there will probably be some such rule. As I've said before, the top executives in the large corporation now propose their own salaries to the board of directors, and these are then ratified by the board which the same executives have themselves appointed. No arm's-length transaction there! It's a very pleasant charade for those involved. Unfortunately for them it is also increasingly being seen as such, and of late our Securities and Exchange Commission has been looking into the matter. One is sad that people cannot indefinitely be fooled by so elegant an arrangement. A negotiated relationship between shop-floor pay and executive pay might be the best form of salary restraint. Following the current French discussion, if a full-time assembly-line worker in the United States got $12,000 a year, then a top executive would have as a ceiling, say, five times as much, or $60,000. That is a living wage.

NICOLE: *It would be a terrific reduction!*

JKG: Make it ten times, or $120,000, then. It's the principle that counts. I only say that executive salaries in the large corporation are extensively influenced by the men who receive them. This means that they must be brought within the scope of the policy – the CIPP, if I can now use the acronym.

NICOLE: *But wouldn't such limits damage incentive? What would be the incentive then?*

JKG: If the man at the top of the enterprise got five or ten times as much as the man at the bottom for an infinitely more pleasant line of work, there would still be a mighty effort to get to the top. But, in any case, corporation executives never claim that there is a relationship between their pay and the work they do. No executive would dream of admitting that he is relaxing on the job, defecting for an occasional afternoon of golf or sex because his pay is too low or his taxes too high. A confession of this kind in the executive dining room would be positively sensational. All corporate executives must praise themselves constantly for the effort they are expending; anything less than the very best is never acceptable. And in most cases they do their best; it's the basic corporate ethic. So, above a certain point, pay has little or nothing to do with incentive. Less income, a simpler life, less pressure to maintain a big house, an expensive family and an excessively decorative wife might actually improve executive productivity and reduce the incidence of heart disease. However, I'm not pressing that point.

NICOLE: *You are really saying that the market has become a kind of disguise for inequality?*

JKG: Absolutely. One of the highest paid of American executives is Mr Meshulam Riklis – he got $915,866 in total compensation in the year ending January 1976. That was the reward of the market. And, alas, his firm, Rapid-American Corporation, was doing very badly; the market is good to you whether your company makes money or loses money. In fact, no one can suppose the market has any meaning if it pays Mr Riklis nearly $916,000 for a moderately responsible job that, on the record, he does rather poorly and Cyrus Vance, the Secretary of State, $66,000 for a much more important, difficult and demanding job, which, I judge, he does quite well. And even at Mr Vance's starvation wages there would be no trouble at all finding a replacement for him. I know lots of people who are available. No one ever suggests that were Vance paid more, he would do better. Like the corporation executive, he is also required to do his best, regardless of pay.

NICOLE: *What about the incomes of the shareholders and property owners? Are they left outside?*

JKG: Taxation must be an integral part of the CIPP. It reaches the incomes that are untouched by wage, salary and price restraint. You can't limit the wages of the workers and executives and say to the shareholders, 'Your returns can be as high as good luck or the wise selection of ancestors makes them.' Or similarly leave lawyers, doctors, other professional people, outside. Since these incomes are not readily fixed, the income tax becomes the means by which you bring them into the general system of restraint. This will be seen as fair.

Equity will also be served by relatively stiff inheritance taxes; inherited money enriches no less than salaries. And inheritance taxes also have a favorable effect on incentive. You release the offspring of the rich from the burdens of inherited wealth and encourage them to work hard on behalf of society. In consequence, they become a small but useful addition to the labor force. Instead of just praising the work ethic, the children of the affluent also practice it.

NICOLE: *What about savings under such a policy? Will there be enough for capital needs?*

JKG: There is no serious problem here. By far the largest part of all saving is now by corporations. This would not be adversely affected; profits, we've seen, would be in line with past experience. A large share of personal savings – savings by and for individuals – is in the form of social insurance and pension funds. These would also be unaffected. And if people know their personal savings will not suffer in purchasing power as a result of inflation, this might be an added incentive to save.

NICOLE: *What about your own book royalties?*

JKG: A very sensitive issue. I would not wish to see them fixed in total amount, for what I didn't get, the publisher would simply get instead, and that would make me deeply unhappy. But neither should I escape. I could survive on less. So my income, like that of doctors, lawyers and other self-employed, should be brought within the CIPP through the tax system – by means of an income tax that, in the upper brackets, is far more steeply progressive than now.

NICOLE: *And you would write fewer books?*

JKG: No, much as that might be welcomed. It's the pride of the corporation executive that he gives his best to his job; it's my curious vanity that I write for the satisfaction as much as for the income. So with most writers, I believe.

NICOLE: *Doesn't this policy tend to freeze everybody at the same relative level of income?*

JKG: Yes and no. You start from where you are. But the bargaining will only be workable and the results defensible if lower incomes gain, over time, at the expense of higher incomes. This is a very practical matter. A general grading up of the lower and middle incomes in relation to higher ones is in line with popular aspirations and helps also to ensure the support of the unions. Union support, in turn, is vital to the success of the policy. In the past there has been a strong suspicion that income restraint has worked better for wages covered by union contracts than for other kinds of income.

NICOLE: *A more equitable income distribution is now more a functional than a moral question?*

JKG: Absolutely.

NICOLE: *Won't the wealthy object?*

JKG: Yes, quite a lot. But you must remember that social tranquillity at all times and in all countries is always advanced by the cries of anguish of the affluent. They have a much deeper sense of personal injustice than the poor and a far greater capacity for indignation. And when the poor hear the primal screams of the well-to-do, they imagine that the fortunate are really suffering and become more contented with their own lot. Good statesmanship has always required not only the comforting of the afflicted but the afflicting of the comfortable.

NICOLE: *How do you bring so many groups together to achieve a consensus?*

JKG: It will require effort and patience. But the numbers are not so great. People have achieved control over their incomes through organization – corporations, unions, farm federations, white-collar groups. The negotiation and administration of a CIPP is possible because these organizations are in workable numbers – in the United States a couple of thousand corporations, a few hundred unions, a handful of farm organizations, representatives of a relatively small number of other groups. And where enforcement is involved, it is of prices and incomes that are now fixed or negotiated.

NICOLE: *This is your earlier point. You are not replacing the market, only acting where it no longer functions?*

JKG: Yes. Where the market works, you keep hands off. You don't touch the prices of the millions of small firms, of the self-employed, of farmers, except as minimums are set by the government. All this enormously simplifies the task.

NICOLE: *Now I come, surely, to the most important question of*

*all. Is it realistic to expect this kind of self-restraint and social
understanding in a highly individualistic, democratic country?*

JKG: We had better hope so because the present isn't good
enough, and, as we've seen, the other remedies are as bad as the
disease, at least for the poor.

Let me remind you, once more, why we are making this
effort. We now restrain prices and wages and other incomes by
slack in the economy – by the restraining effect of low demand,
idle capacity, high unemployment. With the direct restraints
here proposed, people can be put to work and plants can work
at capacity with a greatly reduced risk of inflation. The direct
CIPP restraints would replace unemployment as the basic
policy against inflation.

But to get back to your question. There is nothing so exceptional about this design. It's precisely the direction in which all
of the advanced industrial countries are moving – or maybe
stumbling. Germany and Austria have been working along
these lines for years. Trade union claims are worked out there
in accordance with what can be afforded within the existing
price structure and what will keep costs from driving up
prices. There is then an understanding that employers will not
take advantage of restraints. And other claims are kept in line.
Taxation is seen, if somewhat imperfectly, as an equalizing
factor for other incomes. The Germans and the Austrians have
a name for the whole effort – Social Market Policy. They have
had less inflation and less unemployment than most other
countries. It is this policy that has made the German mark
such a strong currency. Helped by very cooperative unions,
Swiss policy has gone along similar lines. In Switzerland both
inflation and unemployment have been very low.

However, the British may well be nearer to a formal solution
than any other country. They have seen very clearly how uncontrolled efforts to expand incomes shove up prices, how much
unemployment is then needed to restrain the increase, and
what a devastating effect monetary policy has on investment.

So they now have a formal system of wage and price restraints which is still fragile but which reflects the combination of negotiation and compulsion I just outlined. These direct restraints are supplemented by a tax system which keeps higher incomes under equitable restraint and makes concessions, as necessary, to those at the bottom. There are even the outraged screams that give the poor the right feeling of sympathy for the rich. And the British economy has been responding to this policy. Inflation is down; the employment prospect, as we speak, is improving. Furthermore, as we've said, the British do count their unemployed.

NICOLE: *What is being done in France and the United States?*

JKG: The same policy was reflected in Monsieur Barre's control of prices and is still reflected in his control of incomes. In economics France usually does what is practical with a minimum of debate on the underlying theory. France has been coming around to a pragmatic form of CIPP without anyone quite recognizing what is happening.

The United States is a more difficult case. We have far more people who believe in the mystique as distinct from the reality of the market. We also have more economic theology than any other country. For such theologians the market is a sacred thing – it is that in which they believe and what they teach. So we have more people than other countries do who cling to the past.

But, even with us, there is movement. Elementary discussions between government, labor and business leaders have recently been under way. They haven't taken any practical form; they do accept, in principle, the solution I've been urging. Mr Carter's economists, as they preside over the continuing combination of inflation and unemployment, are under increasing pressure. People ask if so much scholarly competence is needed for so poor a result.

Recently, under the leadership primarily of the black community, although many others joined in, the President endorsed the principle of the so-called Humphrey-Hawkins bill. This is a bill without much specific content which commits the President to reducing the level of unemployment to 4 percent by 1983. It was opposed initially by the President's economists; they were forced to argue, in effect, for the continuing use of unemployment as an inflation remedy. This was not very agreeable. And if unemployment is not available as a policy against inflation, even economists have to look for other lines of defense. That is the reason – one reason – I supported Humphrey-Hawkins.

And my economist friends are coming around. Not long ago a senior Establishment figure, Dr Arthur Okun of the Brookings Institution, one of President Johnson's principal economic advisers, reached the end of his patience. He has begun to argue that the old policies have run out, that economists can no longer defend the present combination of inflation and unemployment. Okun has called for tax incentives to union members who hold wage claims to predetermined amounts and to corporations that keep their prices stable. I don't believe this is strong enough – one needs a stick along with a carrot – and he confines himself to the wage/price spiral, which is only a part of the problem. But such proposals accept my present case – that fiscal and monetary policy no longer serve.

I mention Dr Okun as a recent convert. A much earlier one is Professor Sidney Weintraub of the University of Pennsylvania, who has long urged that tax incentives and tax penalties be used for holding the income line. Professor Weintraub and Professor Paul Davidson of Rutgers University are editors of a new journal devoted to these matters, the *Journal of Post Keynesian Economics*.

The high priest of British market orthodoxy for half a century has been Professor Sir John Hicks. Sir John has now come to accept that income claims cause inflation and therefore must be restrained. Another gratifying apostasy.

NICOLE: *Professor Friedman hasn't accepted this principle?*

JKG: Not Professor Friedman. He is a brave man with the courage to say, 'Let history pass me by.' And he will not be alone.

NICOLE: *You say there is danger that measures such as Okun's will arouse high hopes and then be too weak.*

JKG: Yes, I worry about that. It is always easier and wiser in economic policy to retreat from a great effort than to go on from a small one. And economists are terribly susceptible to watered-down banality. President Ford wanted to fight inflation with WIN buttons – WHIP INFLATION NOW. And he established a highly fraudulent body in the Executive offices called the Council on Wage and Price Stability. Its only function was to watch things go wrong. Scholars who could not resist the appeal of public office lent their names to this ludicrous charade. They should have greeted it only with raucous and obscene laughter. Of late, though, some new hands have been urging my case very lucidly. We must be clear: we face a formidably difficult task, involving all groups that have taken control of their incomes and prices.

NICOLE: *Doesn't this policy lead to another cumbersome bureaucracy?*

JKG: Few things can be accomplished without people. However, as I said earlier, the concentration of power that destroyed the market and made a CIPP necessary has also reduced the number of organizations with which the government must deal. It means regulating incomes that are already regulated by a few hundred unions and prices that are already regulated by a thousand or so corporations. There are a limited number of public bodies that now set farm prices, transportation costs, minimum wages. I don't think the additional bureaucracy need be all that large. Nothing certainly on the wartime scale.

NICOLE: *Now, once again, how would the Comprehensive Incomes and Prices Policy help reduce unemployment?*

JKG: You would no longer be using unemployment to restrain prices and incomes and thus to check inflation. That is what CIPP and its enforcement would now do. This accomplished, much more could be done for the unemployed. In the United States more jobs could be given to the young, black, unskilled, without intensifying the inflationary spiral. It comes down to yet another of those wonderfully obvious propositions that would have rejoiced the Coolidge soul: if you are not using unemployment to prevent inflation, you can operate the economy much closer to full employment without inflation.

NICOLE: *One final question. Is CIPP forever?*

JKG: Yes. So long as unions, corporations, farmers, others, exist and struggle successfully for higher prices and incomes.

Chapter 9
The International Scene

NICOLE: *Can any country solve its economic problem by itself? Aren't all countries greatly interdependent? And let me ask another question: why have currencies become so unstable in these last years? The dollar, the franc, the pound are always moving up or down in their exchange value, one for the other.*

JKG: Interdependence is great and growing. Imports and exports are very important in the lives of all people in the industrial countries. And prices of both imports and exports are determined outside any given country or by movements in exchange rates. But a country's own inflation is the place to begin. If prices rise at different rates in different countries – the present situation – then exchange rates are certain to be unstable. If the inflation rate is very high in Britain, as it was until recently, then the pound goes down to compensate or more than compensate. That's because when British prices go up in relation to prices in other countries, people stop buying British goods and traveling in Britain. Sterling, not being wanted, then declines in relation to francs or dollars. That restores the situation. A good thing, too; otherwise no British goods would be sold at all. On the other hand, if prices are comparatively stable, as they have been in Switzerland, then the currency, in this case the Swiss franc, will be in demand to buy goods and travel. The franc gains in value in relation to other currencies. That makes Switzerland and Swiss products expensive for outsiders. And again a good thing, for otherwise everyone would be in Switzerland buying more watches than even the Swiss could make.

This isn't the whole explanation. The Swiss franc has also been strong because Switzerland seeming to be a secure and reliable place, people have been using it as a safety deposit box. So when people from the Arab countries buy Swiss francs, that bids up the franc yet more, makes it even stronger and more than compensates for the stable prices.

In recent years countries that have been heavy importers of oil, the United States among them, have, in consequence, had large accumulations of their money (or its equivalent) in foreign hands – the money that paid for the oil. As foreigners have sought to get rid of the accumulations or convert them to other currencies, this has caused the currency in question to decline in exchange value. But, broadly speaking, currencies have been unstable because of inflation and specifically because inflation has been at different rates in the different industrial countries.

NICOLE: *What is a floating currency?*

JKG: The term is a fraud. Economists and central bankers invented the reference to floating currencies when instability in the exchanges became inevitable. With prices rising at different rates in different countries, there was no chance for stability in the rate at which different currencies were exchanged. That was inconvenient. But what was inevitable and inconvenient could be improved by giving it a better name. So, instead of speaking of currency instability or unpredictability or disorder or chaos, the term 'floating currency' was invented. The public heard the monetary experts and authorities speaking with wonderful solemnity of 'the float' and imagined that they had found something new. They hadn't. They were in a bad storm and called it atmospheric ventilation.

NICOLE: *Is stabilization possible? Isn't that what we mean by international monetary reform?*

JKG: Monetary reform does mean some kind of stable exchange relationship between currencies. But it will not happen so long as inflation continues in the industrial countries. The price increases will be at different rates, and exchange rates will make compensatory adjustments. So when next you hear that the great men of the International Monetary Fund and the U S Treasury, the Federal Reserve System, the Bank of England, the Bank of France, the Bank for International Settlements at Basle and other assorted gnomes are meeting on international monetary reform, you can be absolutely sure that nothing will happen unless, miraculously, inflation in the various countries concerned has first been brought under control. The great men will greatly enjoy seeing each other; they will speak admiringly of each other's wisdom as only bankers can; they will go to quite good restaurants. The Chairman of the Federal Reserve will come out to talk to the press looking very solemn, and the reporters will all swarm around him and say, 'Sir, could you tell us how the meeting went this morning?' He will think carefully and say, 'No comment.' The reporters will assume that great things were decided.

NICOLE: *What was the 'snake' and why did it go to pieces?*

JKG: The 'snake', which goes back to 1972, tied the various European currencies together into what was hoped would be a fairly stable exchange relationship, one with the other. It then provided that all would fluctuate together in relation to the dollar. But there were different rates of inflation in the different European countries – in the different segments of the 'snake'. So the 'snake' broke apart – a painful thing, I'm told, for any snake. The countries with a higher rate of inflation eventually had to allow their currencies to depreciate in relation to the currencies of those with a lower rate. It's an outcome that should have been foreseen; in fact, if I may be allowed a word of self-praise, I did, along with some others, foresee it. I told an exceptionally favored audience of Zurich bankers two or three years ago that it would happen.

NICOLE: *What about the International Monetary Fund – doesn't it stabilize currencies? If not, what does it do exactly?*

JKG: The I M F was created in the closing months of the Second World War and was largely the design of two men, John Maynard Keynes and Harry Dexter White of the United States Treasury. White was a highly intelligent economist who died a little later of a heart attack after he had been accused of being a Communist. It was an improbable charge; good Communists don't spend their time creating things like the International Monetary Fund.

The Fund is essentially a bank which lends to countries that, at the going exchange value of their currency, are having trouble exporting enough goods to earn the money they need to pay for imports and meet their debt obligations. It provides what are essentially stop-gap loans until better control of inflation, devaluation or some stroke of good fortune, such as the finding of oil by the British, allows the country to balance outgo with income again. Along with the loans, it also tenders highly unpopular advice on controlling inflation – advice which invariably includes a recommendation for a cutback in public expenditures. And, increasingly, it makes its loans conditional on accepting such advice. It's a rather large power in international economic affairs. A few weeks ago I went to Mexico to give some lectures, visit friends and respond to the invitation of the new president, who had just been inaugurated. There were news reports that I had been there as a secret agent of the I M F. A very bad thing, I discovered, much like the C I A.

NICOLE: *Could you give a practical example of its operations – the IMF, I mean, not the CIA?*

JKG: The recent British experience provides a good illustration. Since the Second World War, the British have been having difficulty buying food and raw materials, including oil, and servicing their debt. Their manufactured goods were expensive; their industries were not as reliable on delivery dates and quality as those of their German or other competitors. In 1975–6, the pound fell, but it took time for this to have an effect on exports, and it also raised prices of imported goods and added to living costs. So Britain borrowed heavily from the International Monetary Fund. And, in keeping with IMF conditions, it had to make some budget cuts. It also got its wages and prices under better control. Presently the British were selling more in relation to what they were buying, and oil was flowing from under the North Sea more rapidly than anyone had expected. Foreigners began investing again in Britain. Englishmen stopped trying so hard to get their money into dollars and other currencies. Dollars and other foreign-currency balances accumulated in London, and it became possible to pay back loans. This is how the IMF smooths over temporary difficulties, a useful thing. The economic advice is sometimes less useful; it runs to rather righteous warnings against being too generous to the poor. The IMF does not, I promise you, provide any permanent cure for currency instability. That cure will come only when inflation in all major countries is under control.

NICOLE: *If we agree that internal stabilization will come in different ways for different countries, what happens in the meantime?*

JKG: Exchange instability will continue. The currencies of those countries with a low rate of inflation will gain in exchange value. Countries with a high rate of inflation, which are having more trouble in developing the CIPP of which I spoke last time, will see their currencies go down.

NICOLE: *Does that mean that if the United States is slow in developing an incomes and prices policy, your CIPP, the dollar will be weak?*

JKG: Yes. And we need to get our oil imports under control, too.

NICOLE: *But is any international stabilization really possible until the United States stabilizes its prices?*

JKG: Stabilization by the United States is decisively important, for we are a major factor in world trade. If prices in the United

States are stable, a very large segment of all world trade is at stable dollar prices. Also, if dollars are stable, people will be willing to hold them and not try to get them into other currencies. That is an additional source of stability.

Further, if prices are stable in the United States and employment is good, other countries have a fixed point around which to shape their own policies. They can adjust to what they know will happen here. If their prices seem to be low and they are accumulating dollars, it will be an indication that they can let their wages and prices go up a bit, be a little more generous in the income they dispense. And if they are losing dollars, it will be a sign that their prices are too high, that they must keep a firmer hold on wages and other income. If there are inflation and unemployment in the United States and no one knows how much more to expect, economic management in other countries becomes much more difficult. So I attach great importance to stable prices and stable high employment in the United States. Every sensible Frenchman or Frenchwoman should worry first about what Washington is doing and after that think about what is going on in Paris. In a rational world, all finance ministers of all the industrial countries would sit in on President Carter's meetings on economic policy.

NICOLE: *Isn't it unhealthy, even from the standpoint of an American, for so much to turn on American policy?*

JKG: Certainly. The world would function much better with a strong, unified European community able effectively to express and implement its ideas on prices and employment. A second point of view always has a useful corrective influence. Also, our presidential system introduces a discontinuity – a period of change and learning every four or eight years. A strong, articulate Europe would help overcome the effects of this recurrent lapse into on-the-job training.

NICOLE: *But Europe is still a long way from being united.*

JKG: A desire for unity certainly exists. The substance involves a lot more than the rhetoric of international cooperation usually implies. It requires a common fiscal and monetary policy, similar action on prices, wages and incomes, and this probably means a common government with power to adopt and enforce these measures. Only when one has all of these things can one have a common currency. All this is still considerably in the future.

NICOLE: *A minimum degree of cooperation is still useful, is it not?*

JKG: Oh, yes. For example, the development of a CIPP along the lines I outlined will be easier or more difficult as all have a common understanding of the goal and work in harmony to effect it. Then the price movements in one country are not so disruptive a force in others.

NICOLE: *Until Europe develops a common policy, must it adjust to a fluctuating American economy? It will be American and not European stability that counts?*

JKG: American stability will be more important. But that shouldn't be an excuse in Europe for not trying. Our sins are great, but not everything should be blamed on us.

NICOLE: *Won't the prices charged by the OPEC countries and the other raw material producers be a continuing source of instability?*

JKG: Oil prices surely are. But oil may be sui generis – a special case. When the oil cartel escaped from the rule of the market, we immediately thought about similar possibilities for wheat, copper, rubber, cocoa, marijuana and other basic materials. In fact, it isn't nearly so easy to run an international commodity agreement as is sometimes imagined. The oil cartel worked primarily because two countries, Saudi Arabia and Libya, were willing to accept reduced sales in return for the high prices. In the case of most other products, no one country wants to accept the reduction in sales and the resulting accumulation of inventories that, more or less inevitably, go with higher prices. So it cuts prices a little to keep its share of the market or maybe increase its share a little. Others then hear of or suspect the price-cutting and do the same. The chiseling increases, becomes epidemic and the agreement breaks down. This has been the general history of commodity agreements. At most they accomplish only with extreme difficulty what a modern industrial oligopoly does so normally and naturally.

NICOLE: *How upsetting is the high oil price? Isn't it an important cause of inflation?*

JKG: The worst feature is the very different impact on the external expenditures of different countries. Italy, for example, has great difficulty selling enough to pay for the oil for its big automobile population as well as for industrial and heating needs. Likewise Spain. In France it isn't easy. And the less-developed countries that have no oil but are sufficiently developed to use a great deal of it have been in serious trouble. They have been covering the cost of their oil purchases – and also other import needs – with bank loans, including loans from the large American banks. American banks in 1976 had loans to those countries of around $45 billion and, in the case of Brazil, Peru, Zaire and some others, a good deal of worry about possible loss.

NICOLE: *Is this serious?*

JKG: Not desperate. People who lend money must expect on occasion to lose money, and losses can be disguised. The debtor never wants it known that he has defaulted. The creditor never wants it known that he has made a foolish loan. So they get together in a conspiracy of concealment. They speak of extension, rolling over, refinancing, moratoria – all euphemisms for default. In the months and years ahead there will also be pressure on the IMF, the US government, other governments and other public bodies to lend money to the poor countries. This, of course, will help them meet their debt service. We will again see that wonderful flexibility of the capitalist mind. The Citibank in New York is one of the big creditors. Mr Walter

Wriston, its chairman, has long been contending for the world's record for speeches on the purity of private enterprise. But he will be rather tolerant of socialism where public aid to the debtor countries is involved. Or so I predict.

NICOLE: *Haven't some countries worked out their oil problems?*

JKG: Yes. Japan, which has no oil, has sufficiently overcome the price increase so that it again has a big surplus of export revenue over payments. In Germany and Switzerland the process of accommodation is more or less complete. Exports have been increased; domestic use of oil has been held down in some cases.

NICOLE: *What is the prospect on oil prices?*

JKG: In the immediate future there could well be enough new oil around – from the North Sea, the North Slope, Mexico – so that the OPEC countries will be somewhat cautious about raising prices. But I do not know.

I can only let you in on a geological secret. The earth really turns on a great lubricating seal of oil about a mile down. If you drill deeply enough, you tap into that lubricant. The signal that we are exhausting our oil will be a loud squeaking sound under Riyadh. I offered that hypothesis in a speech in Washington once, and the ambassador from one of the OPEC countries, I later learned, cabled it home as a fact. So it must be true.

NICOLE: *Would it have helped us to have been able to foresee the quadrupling of the price of crude oil at the end of 1973?*

JKG: Oh, sure. In the United States we, for a long while, limited oil imports by quotas in order to sustain our own prices, the effect being, of course, that we used up our own supplies. If we had foreseen OPEC and been sensible, we would have relied much more on imported oil and saved our own for the future. Now, of course, our reliance on foreign oil is increasing – up from around 35 percent of consumption at the time of the Arab boycott in 1973 to about half in 1977.

NICOLE: *Why weren't you more sensible and foresighted?*

JKG: The American oil companies, large and small, control a certain number of members of the Congress and handle them pretty much as the performers in a puppet show manipulate their puppets. A squeeze here, a squeeze there and the arms respond and the voice squeaks yes. It's very possibly the greatest scandal in our political life, much more damaging to the public interest than Watergate.

However, the need for foresight is not peculiar to oil. It should now be accepted practice to keep all the prospective supplies and prices of all major materials under constant review and study, to conserve as needed and to have plans against the day of shortage. As our retreat from the market proceeds, there is no longer any market mechanism that ensures that supply will equal demand at prices people will find tolerable.

NICOLE: *What about your big energy program?*

JKG: It isn't very good. It depends for its effect, broadly speaking, on relatively small differences in prices – slightly higher prices for gasoline, slightly higher prices for big cars, slightly higher rates for large users of energy, a slight price differential in favor of energy sources other than petroleum, quite a lot higher prices to stimulate the production of gas and oil. All experience shows that consumers don't respond much to higher prices of petroleum products, and prices were high enough to stimulate production before. You have seen the effect on consumption in France where prices are very high. A top Iranian official – it was the Shah, if I may drop a name – once told me with some indignation that the government of France now gets more money out of a barrel of oil in taxes than Iran does in the price. Energy conservation in the United States will be minor as long as it depends on small or even sizeable price increases.

Mr James Schlesinger, whom Mr Carter put in charge of the energy program, was a student of economics at Harvard. Somewhere along the line we must have forgotten to tell him about the elasticity of demand and that it can be very low. A bad oversight.

NICOLE: *I understand that we should be cautious in the use of every important material. But aren't coal, solar energy, maybe nuclear energy, substitutes for oil?*

JKG: They are. It's why we should plan intelligently and effectively but without paranoia. The modern economy makes heavy use of materials. But it has also, as you say, great capacity for substitution. During the Second World War, we made real efforts to deny ferro-alloys – the things you mix in with steel – to the Germans. Blockade, pre-emptive buying, bombing, were all used to deny them supplies of chrome, nickel, whatever. The Germans very quickly learned that there were far more possibilities for substitution than had previously been imagined. When we investigated after the war, we learned that they weren't really much hurt – that the cost to them of substitution was far less than the cost of the bombing we used trying to deny them the stuff. If in the 1920s and 1930s we had been told that we would have to do without natural rubber in a war, there would have been panic. Speeches of unimaginable gloom would have been made. Something might even have been done about it, although maybe a Schlesinger would have been invented as a substitute for action. Under the press of stark necessity in 1942, we found quite satisfactory substitutes. We should plan, but it should be an exercise of wisdom, not a form of escapism or an act of desperation.

NICOLE: *Can we go back to the strictly monetary scene? Is there a problem with the Eurodollars and now the petrodollars?*

JKG: These are a symptom rather than a disease. In the sixties and early seventies the United States bought much larger quantities of goods in Europe and elsewhere than it was selling; it also had many more tourists visiting Notre Dame, the Louvre, the Place Pigalle and other centers of culture and rest than there were Europeans visiting the Grand Canyon and

Times Square. In consequence, dollars accumulated in Europe and these were augmented by Americans investing in European enterprises. That is all; the Eurodollars accumulated naturally from Americans buying more than they sold.

Similarly the accumulation of petrodollars. It is the result of the Saudi Arabians, the Libyans and the Emirates selling more oil in Europe than they can find hotels to buy or goods in Marks & Spencer. These big chunks of money, short-term deposits, then move like the armies of Genghis Khan over the known world, bidding up currency prices where they go, causing depreciation in the countries they leave behind. It's an embarrassment, but it's a result, not a cause.

So long as the OPEC countries couldn't spend the European currencies and the dollars they earned, the accumulation of petrodollars was inevitable. But the Iranians, some of the Arab countries and the other OPEC members have learned to spend their money far, far faster than people expected. As this has happened, their contribution to the accumulation has diminished or stopped.

NICOLE: *Does the big expenditure for oil have a depressing effect on the French economy and on employment – and also in the United States? Monsieur Barre, our premier, and President Carter have both said that it costs us heavily in jobs.*

JKG: If we bought, and the OPEC countries did not spend, it would. But as they have learned to spend – and some have truly mastered the art of extravagance – the money comes back for the purchase of machinery, equipment, Cadillacs and, unfortunately, a lot of guns and airplanes. But its net effect is depressing as well as distorting.

NICOLE: *When a currency depreciates, as the pound did recently, that country's products become cheap in the world market. Isn't this a subsidy, a kind of manipulation of exchange rates to improve trade? Some people call it monetary protection.*

JKG: True. Although the effect soon wears off. It takes more of the depreciated currency to buy raw materials, food and other things the country has to import. As these go up in price, manufacturing costs rise, and so does the cost of living. That puts pressure on wages and leads to further rises in costs. So, before long, the products the country has to sell are marked up. The advantage from the depreciation is gone. And not only is the advantage temporary; not many countries now want to encourage and suffer the inflation which is involved. The Swiss and the Germans, as I've said, have chosen to let their currencies appreciate even at considerable cost to their export industries. Swiss watches have been very hard to sell in recent times because they must be purchased in very expensive francs. Swiss hotels and ski resorts have been underpopulated because not only have the Americans, Germans and French found it cheaper to go elsewhere but the Swiss themselves, when they want to go skiing, find French mountains much cheaper than their own.

NICOLE: *So why wouldn't they depreciate a little bit?*

JKG: To depreciate and make it stick, more people must want to sell your currency than to buy. That will be true if your prices have been high relative to those of other countries and foreigners have been selling you goods and not buying. Your currency will be in surplus, and by encouraging the sale of the surplus you can depreciate easily enough. But, if you have had no internal inflation, your currency will have been in demand to buy your goods. And people will seek it to hold. Then there is no accumulation to sell. This being so, though some manipulation is possible, it won't go down very far or for very long in relation to other currencies. The Swiss National Bank can sell Swiss francs and so expand the supply. And it can lend more freely and encourage the Swiss government (with some difficulty, I may say) to run a larger deficit. And wage restraints can be relaxed. Then the Swiss franc will fall in relation to other currencies but only because prices in Switzerland will be rising. Again, you see, the rate of internal inflation is ultimately the controlling factor.

I should add that the will to depreciate is not all that strong. For some years I've been a largely absentee professor at the University of Geneva, at the institute there which concerns itself with international affairs. No question is asked me so often as 'Why can't we let the franc fall a bit?' They could. But so long as the Swiss do not want internal inflation, they can't have much depreciation. The Swiss want also to maintain their reputation as reliable bankers who deal in a currency with reliable purchasing power, and banking is, politically, an extremely influential industry in Switzerland. So the tourist and watch industries have, in some measure, been sacrificed to stable prices.

This, I should tell you, is *my* explanation; it's not a question to which everyone in Switzerland gives a clear answer. But the basic point *is* clear: the temptation to depreciate a currency in order to get a trade advantage is not nearly so great as was once imagined.

NICOLE: *Still, isn't there a chance that currency depreciation could lead to protectionism? We hear a lot about a return to protection.*

JKG: That chance – or danger – exists. In the not distant past the dollar was a bit high in relation to the yen. This and the efficiency of the Japanese caused buyers to swarm into Japan, Japanese goods to pour into the United States. In consequence, there was agitation for tariffs or quotas on Japanese textiles, steel and television sets. It has continued as the yen has gained. But the urge for protection must also be kept in perspective. Much of it now comes from textile or shoe manufacturers, national industries where firms are fairly numerous and small. And from the associated trade unions. Or it comes from older and inefficient national industries, of which steel is the best example. Our steel industry has been drifting into obsolescence for years. And the large firms, as the industry itself recognizes, have been poorly managed – a domain of bureaucratic meatheads. There isn't much agitation for protection by the large international firms, those producing automobiles, chemicals, computers and the like. This brings us back to the role and power of the large transnational corporation. For this firm, operating as it does across national boundaries, tariffs are a nuisance. It wants to produce at the place of greatest overall advantage as regards cost, consumer persuasion, getting what it needs from the government; often it will want to produce in one country, assemble in another. And, as I've said, you will always be less concerned about foreign competition if you own the competitor. But more important than such ownership is the understanding between large transnational firms that prices should not be cut, that to do so is a disaster for all. Oligopolistic understanding operates, as one would expect, across national frontiers. Car or computer people don't engage in cut-throat price competition. So, in an economy dominated by large corporations with international operations, there is built-in insurance against a protectionist revival.

NICOLE: *Does that apply to the Common Market?*

JKG: Yes. The Common Market is a superb illustration of my point. Where does the agitation against the Common Market come from? Almost exclusively from small firms and from farmers in particular. The recent outcry in France against Italian wine imports is a case in point. Fiat, in contrast, knows that it must keep the peace with Renault and Citroën. It wouldn't think it wise to dump its cars at sacrifice prices.

I don't want to carry this point to extremes. Large firms that are inefficient will seek protection. This explains the protectionist instinct of the French steel industry and now of the American steel industry. Our steel companies have just recently been providing us with another excellent example of the flexibility of the free-enterprise mind. They have moved from a stirring demand for freedom from government interference to a passionate demand for government interference in the form of tariffs, quotas, minimum prices on imported steel and even government-guaranteed loans for modernization of their plant.

NICOLE: *I think you are really saying that the large corporation has escaped from the market at home and also abroad, that it has escaped from free trade into its own form of protection!*

JKG: I couldn't say it better. The big transnational or multinational firm has built-in protection from both domestic and foreign competition. So it doesn't need tariffs.

NICOLE: *Raymond Barre has recently said that the world needs organized free trade to offset chaotic economic trade relations. He urges consultation and agreement to regulate trade and ease the impact of changing trade patterns between countries.*

JKG: Organized free trade could mean different things to different people. I'm not sure what Monsieur Barre has in mind. For some it could signify a lot of protection. I'm not so emotionally committed to free trade that I welcome the pain it inflicts on ordinary people. Also, we've seen that the big international corporations have their own built-in protection. The pain inflicted by free trade is felt by smaller firms where the market still works.

NICOLE: *What would you do?*

JKG: If textile imports into the United States from Japan, Taiwan, Hong Kong, are suddenly so large as to cause serious unemployment in the mill towns of the American South, I would negotiate limits on the inflow and allow time for a less painful adjustment. If French wine growers are going broke because of imports of Italian wine, I would again urge arrangements to ease the distress. I imagine that Monsieur Barre has this kind of regulation in mind, steps designed to minimize pain and shock. One should always be suspicious of absolutes; any good economic policy should be open to compromise. And, needless to say, if Taiwan, Hong Kong, China or Japan is better at producing textiles than we are, they should be allowed to do it. They probably will, in any case. The more efficient producer usually triumphs in the long run.

NICOLE: *The producers of raw materials play a very important part in international trade. Are world trade relations shifting in their favor as their products become scarcer or they get better control of their prices? Are they the new rich countries?*

JKG: Well, speaking as an American chauvinist, I certainly hope so. Nobody seems to have noticed that we are the hewers of wood and the haulers of water for the rest of humankind. It's to the United States that the sophisticated world goes for the simple, unexciting products that are then processed by the more refined industries of other lands.

NICOLE: *What do you mean?*

JKG: Where does the world go for bread grains for its bakeries? First of all to the United States. And feed grains to produce its meat and milk? Again the United States. And for soybeans for everything from food to plastics? Again the United States. Where does the raw cotton come from in great volume? The United States. And coal, the oldest and crudest of the industrial products – we send coal all the way to such developed countries as Japan. By all the conventional economic calculations, the United States is the first of the Third World countries. I've long been urging that we should vote that way in the United Nations.

NICOLE: *But you don't export just raw materials.*

JKG: We export raw materials in enormous volume. We also export computers and machine tools and machinery, and our blue jeans and phonograph records are the wonder of the world. We even send out an occasional Cadillac or Lincoln Continental to some OPEC land. But our balance of payments would be in worse condition than now if it weren't for our

Third World products. You will see why I hope that the balance of trade shifts to the favor of the raw-material-producing countries – higher prices for raw materials, lower prices for manufactured and finished products.

NICOLE: *Is that the prospect?*

JKG: I don't think so. The outlook still favors manufactured goods, and for reasons that we have seen. Most manufactured products come from the large corporations. The latter have the intrinsic power in their markets that is given by their size, including the power to control their prices and their costs. Most producers of raw materials and food have no such power or, if they do, they get it only with the assistance of their governments. So the producers of manufactured products will continue to be in a better bargaining position, to have better control over their prices than those from whom they buy. Advantage will continue to be with the large, strong producer of highly processed industrial and manufactured products. We see, incidentally, how much is explained when the large corporation is given its proper place in economic discussion.

NICOLE: *What about the very poor countries like Egypt, India, Bangladesh, those that have no oil, no raw materials? What do they do? Can the rich countries and the IMF and the World Bank help them? Shouldn't the newly rich OPEC countries also help?*

JKG: The World Bank has been a very useful institution – borrowing money in the rich countries, investing in the poor. It has very much earned its keep. And I would like to see more of the oil money invested in the poor countries, although we cannot ask more of Saudi Arabia or Iran than we do of ourselves. But not everything will be solved by capital. That's too optimistic. In India, Egypt, Bangladesh and Pakistan, demography, the relationship of people to land and the age-old accommodation to poverty are the decisive factors. Not much of our discussion of these past days is relevant there. It's a different world.

NICOLE: *Should we be concerned, not from a moral standpoint but from a practical one, with the existence of these pockets of deep poverty in the world?*

JKG: Both morally and from a practical point of view. Where so many suffer from something as painful as poverty, there is surely a moral imperative. And the practical problem is equally urgent. The difference between great wealth and great poverty is the basic source of tension within a country. As the world gets smaller, it will surely be an increasingly serious source of tension between countries.

NICOLE: *I have a couple of small points. The Germans and the Japanese have recently been urged by the United States to stimulate their economies in order to buy more of the world's goods at higher prices and to sell less. Is this the kind of coordination of economic policy that is needed?*

JKG: In a primitive way. But, on balance, the Germans have managed their economic affairs better since the Second World War than the United States has. They are ahead of us in developing an incomes and prices policy. So perhaps we should be seeking advice from them. I would be enchanted to see German economists saying to Mr Carter's scholars, 'Why don't you work out the kind of arrangements between your trade unions and your manufacturers and your other claimants on income that we have?' We Americans need constantly to remind ourselves that to be bigger is not necessarily to be wiser.

NICOLE: *What about France? Isn't there something on which we could instruct you?*

JKG: The French lesson, as I've said, consists in doing what seems most practical and then discovering the philosophical reason after the fact. And, finally, articulating that philosophy with much eloquence. In the post-war years, when the world was still trying to operate with fixed exchange rates, there was a marvelous contrast between the French and the British practice. When internal price movements had made devaluation inevitable, the British would have six months of the most intense discussion. Active parliamentary debates. Learned articles in the *Economist*. Even more learned letters to *The Times*. Incomprehensible discussions in the universities. The French, in contrast, would devalue overnight without any discussion. It could be the better way. Do what seems practical or essential. Talk about it afterward.

Chapter 10

Growth, Power and the Politics of the Market

NICOLE: *You say that inflation and unemployment are caused by the decline in the effectiveness of the market resulting from the increasing power of the big corporations and the trade unions and the ability of other groups to control their own incomes or to get support from the state. Does this power affect government and society in other ways? I should think it would.*

JKG: It does – of course. Economic and political life is a matrix in which each part interconnects with the others and all move together. One test of the validity of an economic or social proposition is whether it appears to fit with everything else. The thrust for economic growth, an example we've seen, fits with the purposes of the technostructure and the leadership of the modern corporation. The reason is straightforward. When the corporation is expanding its sales and increasing its employment, there is more rapid promotion for the members of the technostructure, a more predictable increase in salaries, more people to supervise, more resulting prestige and power. Since everyone is rewarded by growth, it becomes a prime goal of the corporation. And the corporation then converts its goals into public goals. An increasing Gross National Product is a measure of economic and political success because corporate growth is much easier in an expanding economy.

After the Second World War, scholars, politicians, statesmen made the social benefits of economic growth into a religion. When the economy was dominated by the entrepreneurs of neo-classical economics – small tradesmen, farmers, small manufacturers – there was very little talk about economic growth. Good business then meant only good profits. The emphasis on growth developed as the economy and the polity came to be dominated by the large firms. As we've seen, they and their executives benefited greatly from expansion and the associated power, larger salaries, enhanced prestige. Economists came aboard and made a virtue out of a far more fundamental trend.

NICOLE: *Does this celebration of growth assume unlimited natural resources?*

JKG: Initially I think it did. There has always, of course, been some thought that we might run out of important raw materials. In the years following the Second World War, President Truman empaneled a special commission under William S. Paley, the head of the Columbia Broadcasting System for the last century or so, to look into future supplies. The Paley Commission warned that some materials were being used in too prodigal a fashion and would one day be exhausted. Far too much lead was being blown into the air as we burned up gasoline. But nobody paid much attention. Certainly no one suggested that economic growth should be slowed down.

NICOLE: *You raised this question in* The Affluent Society.

JKG: Yes. What little reputation I retain as a Bolshevist, I've often said, comes from having questioned the virtue of unconsidered, unrestrained growth. My concern, though, was not with the exhaustion of our supplies of raw materials – petroleum, metallic ores or what have you. It was with what mindless growth was doing to our surroundings, to the environment. We should, I urged, balance the rewards of growth against the damage to air, water, tranquillity and, above all, the landscape. Men of uncomplicated mind were then saying, in effect, that economic growth solved all problems. Given an adequate rate of growth, a country need not worry about its educational system, its progress in science or technology, even its military strength. All were taken care of by an adequate increase in the Gross National Product. In the later editions of *The Affluent Society*, I dropped out the chapter ridiculing the people, including one or two scholarly warriors from Harvard, who said that national security was ensured by a sufficient rate of economic growth. Once ridiculed, they became silent, and I was then overtaken by compassion. It's the only argument I am reasonably certain that I ever won.

NICOLE: *How do you explain the concern over growth today – the findings of the Club of Rome in 1972 suggesting that we must bring growth to an end? And wasn't this an argument you won?*

JKG: No, much as I might relish the thought. I do suppose *The Affluent Society* helped begin the discussion. But if something affects people's lives and causes anxiety, there is a sensitive nerve there that can be touched. People then react. The first person to touch that nerve gets more credit than he or she deserves. Sooner or later people were certain to see what unconsidered, unplanned economic growth was doing to their air, water, scenery or ears, would see that economic life had a dimension of quality as well as of quantity. I've spoken often of the tactical wisdom of being first with the inevitable.

And there is always a likelihood that any new political movement will go to extremes. I have never quite agreed with the advocates of zero growth. Growth and increasing income ease a good many social problems. People compare their income this year with their income last year, and if they find some improvement, they feel better. Tension is reduced. Were growth to come to an end, income would no longer increase, and the overwhelming question would be 'How is the fixed total to be shared?' For each person's increase there would have to be a decrease somewhere else. Income distribution would become an extremely urgent issue, especially as no society can justify extremes of wealth and poverty, even though the rich and their house philosophers do bring considerable ingenuity and indignation to the effort. But it will be easier and safer if movement toward greater equality can come gradually as reform rather than abruptly as the result of a quarrel over the division of a fixed product.

NICOLE: *Then we should learn how to live with less, or should we?*

JKG: We don't have to learn to live with less overall. We will certainly have a slower rate of growth in the future in the industrialized countries than at times in the past. This is one reason we don't need to be so aroused about the supply of savings and resulting capital for investment.

NICOLE: *Isn't it still necessary to have people who can save – and invest?*

JKG: It was once held that the rich, having more than they could spend, had no choice but to save. So they became social benefactors, the source of capital. The argument was never wholly persuasive – rather like the case for economizing on food by giving a few more than they could eat and starving the rest. But, for a long while, most saving and capital formation had not been by individuals, rich or poor. It has been by corporations out of earnings that they do not distribute to their stockholders.

I earlier mentioned the convergent tendencies of capitalism and socialism. There is another example here. Both modern capitalism and modern socialism agree that if you want income saved, you must keep it out of the hot, eager hands of people who have the choice of spending it. The decision on what to save and what to invest in both systems is made not *by* people but *for* people.

NICOLE: *Was the uprising of students in the sixties and early seventies part of this questioning of growth?*

JKG: I suppose to some extent. In the late sixties students, of whom I used to see a great deal, were in general retreat from the values of the consumer society. One manifestation was the rejection of its manners and dress. Nothing caused my generation such discontent as the sudden abandonment by the young of razors, haircuts and regular bathing and the seeming satisfaction in shabby clothes. But in the United States the Vietnam war and the hot breath of the draft boards were probably more important. They did more than alter attitudes about the consumer society; for a time they even threatened the basic student commitment to sex, alcohol and athletics.

NICOLE: *You make a great point that military spending is an aspect of economic and corporate power.*

JKG: I do, and I would like to say another word on the subject. There is no great disagreement as to the military-economic power. The difference is between those who worry about it and those who avert their eyes or try to justify it. It was Dwight D. Eisenhower, a general and a Republican, who gave us the term 'military-industrial complex' and told us to be vigilant about this unlicensed and uncontrolled power in our society. Much of its influence is exercised for things that are unrelated even to competition with the Soviet Union. In the United States we've long known that the great nuclear aircraft carriers were obsolescent. They would be marginally useful for fighting a non-power such as North Vietnam – for standing offshore to do some salutary and therapeutic bombing. But our enthusiasm for such wars has diminished; if we must move in on, say, Nicaragua, cheaper vehicles would more than serve. In a war with any serious power possessed of missiles, the carriers would be fatally vulnerable, would have to be rushed to the nearest beach and might not make it. But the naval aviators wanted airplanes, and the admirals wanted those lovely big ships, and the aircraft companies wanted to sell the airplanes, and so great was their combined power in the Executive, in the Congress and with the public that no one, for a long while, could touch them. Eventually, however, President Carter was able to announce a cutback in the production of new aircraft carriers.

NICOLE: *But competition with the Soviets is still a real factor. Surely they build weapons too?*

JKG: Oh, yes. The Soviet Union has a powerful bureaucracy which, we must assume, includes a powerful military bureaucracy. Soviet innovations in weapons systems stimulate similar innovations in the United States. A new form of destruction developed in the United States justifies a similar development in the Soviet Union. And we both pass to a higher derivative where we believe the Soviets could do something terrible and so we do it, and, no doubt, the Soviets imagine that we are capable of doing something and so they do it. There is even a seasonal aspect to the whole process. Concern over the Soviet arms build-up always reaches its most alarming level in Washington around the turn of the year, when the new budget is coming up for consideration. It then tapers off until the next surge in the following December or January.

The arms race is important and critical – and potentially fatal. Once we thought it an aspect of the ideological confrontation. Capitalism versus Communism. Now we should see it as an escalating trap. Each side takes the action that the military-industrial complex on the other side most needs to justify the action *it* wants to take. A very high American official – since he's out of office, I can say that it was Henry Kissinger – once told me that you could understand the relations between the Soviet Union and the United States only if you realized that the proponents of military expenditures in both countries had united against the civilians of both countries.

NICOLE: *Can one hope that something will break this vicious circle? Might it be popular opposition, either in the Soviet Union or in the United States? It would have to be in the United States, for people there have more power.*

JKG: It's essential, and maybe it's not a barren hope. Most

people, I judge, want to survive. We've also seen that the pressure for more public and private goods and services is strong. And, though the military power and the corporations work in symbiotic association, they are not all-powerful. We used to believe that when war broke out and the bands began to play and the soldiers to march, all opposition to the conflict would disappear. Or what remained would be put down as unpatriotic, aid to the enemy. So it was during the two world wars. But in Algeria civilian resistance eventually overpowered the commitment of the old French military establishment to the war there. Similarly, thanks to Mendès-France, in Indochina. And the even more spectacular recent case was in the United States. Originally our Cold Warriors took it largely for granted that once we were committed in Vietnam, all the forces of military chauvinism would take over; the country would put its brains on ice for the duration. Instead, to their undoubted surprise and chagrin, there was an increasingly close examination of the reasons we were there. People asked why we were bent on relearning the ghastly lessons of the French experience, why we were so determined to rescue a country from the obscurity that it had devoutly sought, enjoyed and deserved. This questioning extended from the universities to the Congress to the public at large and eventually forced President Lyndon Johnson out of office. Combined with the truly inspired futility of the government we were supporting in Saigon, it forced our withdrawal from Vietnam. The day of the helicopters was not a very graceful event, nothing to stir our national pride. But, remarkably, people mostly put the whole dreadful episode out of their minds. It was bad but better than a bad war.

So popular power can be very great once it's mobilized. There is now great pressure in the United States on behalf of SALT – strategic arms limitation. It is not so flamboyant as the opposition to the Vietnam war or so flagrant in its lobbying as the arms lobby. But it is a very solid, very powerful influence.

NICOLE: *Suppose reason prevails and the enormous amount of money and effort spent for military purposes could be diverted into non-military things like housing, health, education and so on. Would that wreck the economic system? How much adjustment would be necessary?*

JKG: I used to think that the adjustment would be very difficult because the magnitudes are so different. For the cost of a couple of B-1 bombers, any medium-sized city in the United States could build an excellent mass transportation system. But I'm no longer worried. The pressure of civilian needs is greater than we ever imagined. The costs of social insurance, pension systems in particular, in all of the industrial countries are, we are learning, much larger than we ever expected. A major miscalculation. So are the costs of running the modern metropolis, of which New York is the extreme example. Another major miscalculation. And these costs are increased by the influx from the countryside and the poor countries – the modern solution for rural poverty. The new arrivals have an enormous need for housing, education and welfare support. And it takes more money to keep the peace and minimize the friction as people of different backgrounds, races and cultures come together. Beyond all this is the pressure for higher private consumption as people no longer accept that if they work with their hands or are black, they should be poor and live in a mean and nasty way. So I no longer think we would have trouble turning military expenditures to useful civilian purposes. We have also to ask ourselves if some part of this money couldn't be employed helping to increase production and income in the poor countries.

NICOLE: *Shouldn't one be surprised at a government which sends men to the moon and doesn't rescue a city like New York from being bankrupt?*

JKG: I've often said that people sense their own interest and with a little time come strongly to its defense. New Yorkers could be the exception to that useful tendency. They should have risen up in outrage. The services of the city weren't being very efficiently performed. But to cut back on schools, parks, paving, garbage removal and other public services was criminal and the result a national disgrace.

NICOLE: *In this same vein, do scientists and technologists press their goals and defend their personal income?*

JKG: You can bet they do. They could be among the most powerful of all. They have managed to get nearly universal acceptance of the principle that any expenditure which widens the frontiers of knowledge is good and should never be questioned. To wonder about the justification for any scientific outlay produces either an indignant or a condescending response. I am very cautious about such speculation myself. Once or twice I've found myself lacking in curiosity as to the precise chemical, physical, biological or aesthetic content of the lesser gravel in the Saturn ring, wondering whether we should be spending some hundreds of millions of dollars on this instead of reclaiming the worst areas of New York. But at the Harvard Faculty Club I never dream of raising such questions; I know there would only be indignation over my anti-intellectual tendencies. I feel very brave mentioning it now.

Maybe, though, I overstate my case. Recently we have had some cutbacks in space exploration, stopped development of regular passenger service to the moon. There is discussion over where the growth of nuclear technology is taking us and the wisdom of efforts to improve the race genetically, much as a long association with Washington social life suggests the need. Some of my fellow scientists, after a close scrutiny of themselves, have even been led to wonder if the race could be all that much improved. So even in as sacred an area as science and technology, we see anxiety over cost or trend producing the expected countervailing reaction.

NICOLE: *But doesn't science and technology rescue itself from the problems it creates? Science found a way to get useful chemi-*

*cals out of crude oil. So won't scientists find a way to clean the
air that the petrochemical factories have polluted?*

JKG: I'm not entering a general objection to science and technology. I am saying only that it is not exempt from social
process. Wherever you have a position of great political
strength, you generate anxiety over the uses to which that
strength is put. And that applies for scientists as well as for
corporations and the military-industrial complex. A good
thing for all.

NICOLE: *Let me go back to the corporate power in the economy
once more. How does the consumer get managed by the corporation?*

JKG: It has become a very high art, the most studied modern
art form. It's the purpose of marketing research, salesmanship,
advertising, and in the United States it's what finances our
television industry. It's an integral aspect of modern industrial planning. For those who look beyond the myth, it is
one of the clearest manifestations of the convergence of industrial systems – convergence not on the market but on
planning. If General Motors or Ford spends a billion dollars
and several years designing what it calls a new automobile and
brings it into production, it can't leave its sales purely to
chance. It can't be so foolish as to allow the consumer to
exercise his or her sovereign will. That can be permitted in the
economics textbooks but not in the real world. So it must
extend planning to the consumer and ensure that the consumer
will want what it has produced.

NICOLE: *Surely most other economists disagree with this view?*

JKG: Yes, the traditionalists have certainly dug their heels in
on this one – formed a circle with heads in and rumps out like
the buffalo herds under attack in the West. And their instinct
is right, for once you let go of the idea of consumer sovereignty
and concede that the corporation has power on both sides of
the market, you strike a devastating blow at the neo-classical

system. The market really ceases to be an independent power when the large corporation has control, or great influence, over both buyers and sellers. However, I would judge that younger, mentally more accessible scholars do accept the role of advertising, merchandising and consumer management as an aspect of corporate planning.

NICOLE: *Isn't the consumer starting to know better his or her needs and how to resist?*

JKG: Yes. The same familiar process of power begetting an offsetting or countervailing power works here. The management to which the consumer is subject produces resistance. This leads to organization to provide better information, to get legislation ensuring the safety, durability and quality of products and to force disclosure of all exotic, inedible and carcinogenic ingredients. The movement we call consumerism is an admirable example of this tendency for power to develop offsetting power. Ralph Nader, as I may have said, didn't just happen. His movement was born out of the corporate effort to manage the consumer. This the corporations have sensed. General Motors detectives even investigated him a few years ago. They hoped to find something disgraceful – that he secretly watched television commercials or ate non-nutritious breakfast foods.

NICOLE: *And now we have departments of consumer affairs in governments.*

JKG: A manifestation of the same tendency.

NICOLE: *And talk in your country of deregulation of industry.*

JKG: That is the answer of people who feel that the protection of the consumer has gone too far. And some of the talk of deregulation comes from my fellow economists, who are persuaded that this might save the market. There is room for a touch of romance even in economics. The principal proponents are at the Hoover Institution on the campus of Stanford

University and at the American Enterprise Institute in Washington. The Stanford people are very solemn scholars who are trying to recapture the world of Herbert Hoover – it's a very worthy idea, intellectual archaeology as it were. Once aging and righteous scholars of conservative mood dreamed of going to heaven. Now it's to the American Enterprise Institute.

There will, of course, be no general deregulation, and the market will not be redeemed. But I do not criticize the effort; one must understand and even sympathize with people who resist their own obsolescence. They believe it easier to change the world than to change their own ideas. That's natural even if it's not a very practical position.

NICOLE: *Are you somehow saying that all life has become a process of bargaining between opposing power groups?*

JKG: Perhaps not all life but a very great deal of life. Where economic affairs were once regulated by the market, they are now extensively the product of the bargaining between interest groups under the aegis of government. The development of an incomes and prices policy – our CIPP – is the most spectacular and important result of this trend.

NICOLE: *But no matter what group the individual belongs to, isn't he or she first of all and always a consumer? And isn't the goal of your political concert, in the end, to improve the life of the consumer?*

JKG: Not just to consume more but to have the consumption in safer and environmentally more pleasant surroundings which reflect an improved quality of life. But it isn't as simple as that. Most people think of themselves first of all not as consumers but as producers. The members of the technostructure of General Motors, General Electric or Shell think of themselves as manufacturers of automobiles, electrical goods or petrochemicals rather than as consumers of housing, food, medical care or even whiskey. Farmers think of themselves first as producers of cattle, wheat, tobacco, cotton and wine, not as consumers of food, clothing or public services. The blue- or white-collar worker thinks first of his job and pay. And so it goes. Much political economy has to do with advancing and reconciling producer interest. The producer interest is also specific and cohesive while the consumer interest is diffuse and general. So, at a minimum, it takes more time for the consumer interest to mobilize itself and make its concerns felt. Consumers of gasoline or automobiles have to collect money to pay for a lobby in Washington. The producers can turn to a nice big corporate treasury. So the consumer interest is not necessarily decisive in the great bargaining process which economic life has become.

NICOLE: *Does this general bargaining mean that economics is obsolete?*

JKG: Only if it draws an arbitrary line around itself which excludes what is important. If economics is so defined that it depends for its validity on the impersonal operation of the market, then it is obsolete. But it need not be so circumscribed, and with this an increasing number, mostly of younger economists, would agree. A generation back, a reference to neo-classical economics with its commitment to the market was descriptive. Now, for many, it is pejorative. And, for the defenders of the faith, the proof of obsolescence lies not in the arguments of their opponents but in the results of their recommendations. We are, I believe, approaching a time of change in economic policy. But, as we speak, basic policy in the United States – monetary and fiscal policy – still assumes that the market performs according to the neo-classical design, that it hasn't yielded power over prices and incomes to the corporations, unions, farm organizations or other groups with influence in the state. And economists, proceeding on that assumption, are getting the combination of unemployment and inflation that is predictable and that they themselves most deplore. This is the hard and inescapable proof of the obsolescence of the subject when narrowly defined.

Worse still, reliance on the market has become a disguise for injustice which, if intentionally inflicted, not many would defend. No one, or not many, would deliberately accept an arrangement which put the cost of controlling inflation on the young, the unskilled, the minorities or those who are all three. But that is now the effect of relying on monetary and fiscal policy, measures which assume the unimpaired effectiveness of the market.

The market is also our cloak over the exercise of corporate power. Nothing more usefully disguises the power that is exercised by General Motors, Lockheed, Shell, Unilever or Dassault than the continued instruction of the young that all corporate operations are subordinate to the market. In contrast, nothing would so focus attention on corporate power and its consequences for economic management as general classroom instruction and discussion along the lines of our talks of these last few days. Students would emerge from classes with the most inconvenient truths in mind; they would see the inevitability of poor performance if one relies on the market and the absolute necessity for new measures and initiatives if the system is to work properly. So the market is not only obsolete; it is also the servant of those who, for good personal and pecuniary reasons or because of intellectual torpor, wish to keep things as they are, wish to avoid the modern reality.

NICOLE: *Don't we need a name for the people who deal with the new reality?*

JKG: I suppose so. But maybe 'political economist' will do a while longer. The reality is more important than the name.

NICOLE: *Are you depressed?*

JKG: Only at not being young and seeing a chance to be fully involved in the change that lies ahead. The design of a system that reconciles the various claimants on income and devises a workable – and equitable – alternative to the market will be greatly exciting. The battles will be wonderful, the distress of the comfortable extreme. It will be good for political economists; even those who are most contented with their computers, their models of competitive market behavior and their loving wives may be stirred to thought. We know also from the experience of the last hundred years, and especially of the last half century, that the system lends itself to an infinite amount of improvisation and patching up. That I again emphasize. And there can also be great and visible progress in political economy. It will be or can be a lovely time for the profession.

Index